Crypto Fundamentals

Unlocking the World of Cryptocurrencies: Essential Concepts and Strategies

Aiden Stone

Table of Contents

INTRODUCTION

Welcome to "Crypto Fundamentals: Unlocking the World of Cryptocurrencies - Essential Concepts and Strategies." This book will take you on a tour through the intriguing world of cryptocurrencies, demystifying the complicated world of digital currencies and providing you with the knowledge and tactics you need to navigate this fast-changing landscape successfully.

The world's attention has been captured on cryptocurrencies, which are redefining how we think about monetary systems, financial institutions, and technology. Cryptocurrencies were initially an obscure concept, but they have since grown to become a worldwide phenomenon that is altering economies and posing a challenge to established financial institutions. Cryptocurrencies were born out of a desire for financial sovereignty and decentralized governance.

As we continue our exploration of the digital world, the first thing we will do is get a solid grasp on what cryptocurrencies actually are and how they function. We will investigate the innovative technology that underpins cryptocurrencies, known as blockchain, and comprehend the relevance of this technology in terms of safeguarding and confirming transactions across the decentralized network.

We will study the most renowned cryptocurrencies, such as Bitcoin, and learn about alternative digital currencies, often known as altcoins, even though many cryptocurrencies are currently in circulation. In addition, we will go into the world of stablecoins, digital assets that maintain their value over time, as well as utility and security tokens, both of which are utilized in decentralized ecosystems for various purposes.

You will need to be familiar with buying, selling, and trading cryptocurrencies on reputable exchanges to participate in the cryptocurrency world actively. In addition, you will need to know how to set up a cryptocurrency wallet and the significance of public and private keys.

In the world of cryptocurrencies, security is of the utmost significance, and in this book, we will discuss the most effective methods for preserving and protecting your digital assets. We will ensure that your cryptocurrency investments are securely protected, regardless of whether you store them in hardware wallets, software wallets, or the more traditional paper wallets.

Mining is an essential part of many cryptocurrencies; we will explain what it means to mine cryptocurrencies and the many mining techniques currently used in the market. In addition, we will talk about the effects of mining on the surrounding environment and the current debate regarding the industry's viability.

To successfully navigate the cryptocurrency market, you need a keen eye and an awareness of how market movements work. You'll be able to make more informed decisions and better handle the inherent volatility of the cryptocurrency market with our guidance as we share insights into fundamental and technical research.
It is essential, just as it is with any other type of financial effort, to be aware of the legal and tax implications of transactions using cryptocurrencies. We will discuss the worldwide regulatory landscape and provide you with the

knowledge you need to navigate these ideas when we have finished our discussion responsibly.

We will walk you through the steps necessary to construct a diversified cryptocurrency portfolio that is in line with the level of risk you are willing to take and the investing objectives you have set for yourself. We are going to address the benefits and drawbacks of day trading versus holding for a long time, as well as how to strike the best balance between trading and investing.

The utilization of cryptocurrencies is becoming increasingly widespread, which has led to an increase in the number of fraudulent schemes and scams. We will discuss the various prevalent frauds in the cryptocurrency space and offer helpful advice to protect you against con artists.

In the final part of this book, we will look into the future of cryptocurrencies and investigate new trends and technologies that can potentially alter the sector. In addition, we will discuss the opportunities and difficulties that may come our way as we go into the revolutionary digital frontier.

Are you prepared to plunge into the exciting world of cryptocurrencies? Let's get started on this informative adventure together so that I may provide you with the information and tactics you need to navigate the fascinating and ever-changing world of cryptocurrencies successfully!

CHAPTER I

The Basics of Cryptocurrency

Brief history of cryptocurrencies

Cryptocurrencies, the digital marvels that have captivated the world, emerged as a radical solution to age-old financial challenges. The idea of digital cash was conceptualized in the 1980s, with pioneers like David Chaum exploring the concept of secure and anonymous electronic transactions. However, it was not until 2008 that a breakthrough occurred when an individual or group operating under the pseudonym Satoshi Nakamoto published the whitepaper for Bitcoin, the first decentralized cryptocurrency. Nakamoto mined the first-ever "genesis block" block on January 3, 2009, setting the stage for a global financial phenomenon.

In its early days, Bitcoin attracted a small community of tech enthusiasts, cypherpunks, and those seeking an alternative to traditional financial systems. Mining Bitcoin and supporting the network required minimal computational power. As the community grew, the value of Bitcoin rose, and its use as a medium of exchange became more prominent. The success of Bitcoin paved the way for numerous alternative cryptocurrencies, known as altcoins, such as Litecoin, Ripple, and Ethereum. Each brought its unique features and use cases, expanding the possibilities of blockchain technology beyond financial transactions.

The rapid growth of cryptocurrencies also brought challenges. In 2014, the infamous Mt. Gox exchange suffered a devastating hack, losing over 850,000 Bitcoins. This event exposed the vulnerability of centralized exchanges and underscored the importance of secure storage and robust security measures.

As cryptocurrencies gained traction, governments and financial regulators worldwide took notice. Concerns about illicit activities and money laundering initially led to skepticism, but eventually, some countries recognized cryptocurrencies as a legitimate asset class. Japan, for example, officially recognized Bitcoin as legal tender in 2017, bolstering the credibility of cryptocurrencies.

The Initial Coin Offerings (ICOs) rise in 2017 led to an unprecedented boom in the cryptocurrency market. While some ICOs were successful, many were scams or unviable projects, leading to the ICO bubble bursting in 2018. This event raised questions about the sustainability of certain fundraising methods and emphasized the importance of due diligence.

In the years following the ICO bubble, the cryptocurrency market matured. Bitcoin solidified its position as digital gold and a store of value, while other projects focused on real-world use cases and technological advancements. Institutional interest in cryptocurrencies grew, with major financial institutions and corporations entering the space. Cryptocurrency derivatives, futures contracts, and custody services further bolstered the credibility of digital assets.

Decentralized Finance, or DeFi, emerged as one of the most significant trends in the cryptocurrency space. DeFi platforms offered a wide range of financial services without traditional intermediaries, showcasing the potential for blockchain technology to disrupt and innovate in the financial sector.

Looking ahead, the trajectory of cryptocurrencies remains uncertain but filled with promise. Governments continue to explore regulations, technological advancements like Ethereum 2.0 promise scalability and efficiency, and central bank digital currencies (CBDCs) aim to revolutionize traditional fiat systems. With the potential to encourage fresh innovation and build a more inclusive, decentralized, and equitable financial future, cryptocurrencies are set to become a more major part of the global financial landscape.

In conclusion, the history of cryptocurrencies has been a tumultuous journey of innovation, adoption, challenges, and resilience. From the invention of Bitcoin to the rise of diverse altcoins and the market's maturation, cryptocurrencies have evolved into a transformative force in the modern world. As we move forward, it is essential to learn from the past, embrace innovation responsibly, and harness the power of cryptocurrencies to create a more inclusive, decentralized, and equitable financial future.

Importance of understanding cryptocurrency basics

With its disruptive power over traditional finance and revolutionizing our understanding of money and transactions, cryptocurrencies have come to prominence. Understanding cryptocurrency basics is essential for individuals and businesses alike, as it empowers them to navigate this rapidly evolving landscape, make informed decisions, and unlock the numerous opportunities and benefits of digital currencies.

Blockchain technology, an immutable, decentralized ledger that records transactions over a network of computers, is the cornerstone around which cryptocurrencies are based. Because of this technology, which ensures transparency, security, and trust, there is no longer a requirement for intermediaries which include banks and other financial institutions. By grasping the fundamental concepts of blockchain and its role in cryptocurrencies, individuals can appreciate the potential for financial inclusion, reduced transaction costs, and enhanced security.

One of the most compelling reasons to understand cryptocurrency basics is the financial empowerment it offers to individuals. Cryptocurrencies enable financial sovereignty, allowing people to control their wealth without reliance on traditional banking systems. Cryptocurrencies provide access to international markets and business opportunities in areas with restricted banking services availability. Knowing how to set up and secure a cryptocurrency wallet lets users store, send, and receive digital assets directly, giving them complete control over their funds.

Moreover, understanding cryptocurrency basics is crucial for investing in this emerging asset class. The cryptocurrency market is highly dynamic and often subject to significant price fluctuations. Educated investors can analyze projects, assess their potential, and identify sound investment opportunities. Additionally, comprehending concepts such as market capitalization, trading volumes, and technical analysis equips investors with the tools to make calculated and strategic investment decisions, mitigating risks associated with volatile markets.

For businesses, integrating cryptocurrencies can bring a host of benefits, including faster and cheaper cross-border transactions, increased accessibility to global customers, and innovative fundraising methods. Businesses that grasp cryptocurrency basics can explore opportunities to accept cryptocurrencies as payment, gaining a competitive edge and appealing to a tech-savvy customer base. Furthermore, businesses can explore the potential of blockchain technology in supply chain management, data security, and enhancing customer
trust.

Understanding the significance of blockchain and cryptocurrencies is also vital for policymakers and regulators. As digital currencies gain traction, governments face the challenge of creating appropriate regulatory frameworks that protect consumers while fostering innovation. Policymakers well-versed in cryptocurrency basics can strike a balance between embracing innovation and mitigating potential risks, ensuring that the technology can flourish while maintaining a secure and stable financial ecosystem.

The importance of understanding cryptocurrency basics extends beyond the financial realms. Blockchain technology holds potential in various sectors, such as healthcare, voting systems, intellectual property rights, etc. By grasping these concepts, researchers and professionals can explore novel use cases and contribute to developing blockchain solutions that benefit society.

Cryptocurrency basics also encompass cybersecurity awareness. With the rise of digital assets, cyber threats have increased as well. Understanding best practices for securing private keys, recognizing phishing attempts, and utilizing secure wallets can safeguard individuals from falling victim to cybercriminals seeking to exploit the crypto ecosystem.

Moreover, grasping cryptocurrency basics fosters an informed and educated community, reducing the prevalence of misinformation and misconceptions. As cryptocurrencies continue to gain mainstream attention, having accurate knowledge enables individuals to engage in constructive conversations, contributing to the broader adoption and acceptance of digital currencies.

In conclusion, understanding cryptocurrency basics is paramount in today's rapidly evolving financial landscape. Grasping the concepts of blockchain, decentralized systems, and digital currencies empowers individuals, businesses, policymakers, and researchers to unlock the vast potential of this transformative technology. Whether seeking financial empowerment, investment opportunities, innovative business strategies, or societal advancements, knowledge of cryptocurrency basics paves the way for a more inclusive, efficient, and secure future.

CHAPTER II

What are Cryptocurrencies?

Definition of cryptocurrencies

Cryptocurrencies have emerged as a groundbreaking concept, disrupting traditional financial systems and reshaping how we transact, invest, and perceive value. Fundamentally, a cryptocurrency is a digital or virtual currency that verifies asset transfers, controls the creation of new units, and secures transactions by applying cryptographic principles. Understanding the definition of cryptocurrencies is essential for anyone seeking to navigate the rapidly evolving landscape of digital currencies and harness their transformative potential.

Blockchain technology is at the heart of any cryptocurrency, which serves as the underlying infrastructure. A blockchain is an immutable and decentralized ledger that keeps track of every transaction made through a network of computers called nodes. Every block in the chain has a list of transactions, and a chain of blocks is created using cryptographic hashing, which connects each new block to the one before it. This design ensures that the entire transaction history is transparent, traceable, and tamper-resistant, as altering any information within a block would require changing all subsequent blocks, a computationally infeasible task.

The emergence of this ground-breaking technology was marked in 2009 by the launch of Bitcoin, the first cryptocurrency. Created by an individual or group operating under the pseudonym Satoshi Nakamoto, Bitcoin aimed to provide a peer-to-peer electronic cash system that did not rely on intermediaries such as banks. Bitcoin's blockchain allows participants to transfer funds directly to each other securely, pseudonymously, without the need for traditional financial institutions.

The most crucial feature of cryptocurrencies is decentralization, meaning they are not controlled or regulated by any central authority. In contrast to conventional currencies, which are managed and issued by central banks and governments, cryptocurrencies are run by global networks of decentralized nodes. This lack of central control confers various advantages, including increased transparency, resistance to censorship, and the potential to foster financial inclusion for individuals who lack access to traditional banking services.

In addition to Bitcoin, thousands of alternative cryptocurrencies, commonly called altcoins, have emerged. Each altcoin typically operates on its own blockchain or, in some cases, as a token on an existing blockchain platform. These alternative cryptocurrencies often introduce unique features, use cases, or improvements over Bitcoin's original design. Some examples of notable altcoins include Ethereum, which introduced smart contracts and decentralized applications (DApps), and Ripple, which focuses on fast and low-cost cross-border payments.

The issuance and supply of cryptocurrencies are governed by specific rules programmed into their respective protocols. Most cryptocurrencies have a capped supply, meaning a predetermined maximum number of coins will ever exist. For instance, Bitcoin's maximum supply is limited to 21 million coins. This scarcity attribute is intended to mimic the scarcity of precious metals like gold, making cryptocurrencies attractive to those seeking a store of value.

Cryptocurrencies achieve security through cryptographic principles. Public-key cryptography is employed to generate a cryptographic keys pair: a public key, which is shared openly and serves as an address for receiving funds, and a private key, which is kept secret and used to sign transactions for spending funds. Cryptographic keys ensure that only the holder of the private key has control over the associated cryptocurrency assets, adding an additional layer of security to the network.

Cryptocurrencies employ various consensus mechanisms to facilitate transactions and ensure consensus across the network. Bitcoin, the first cryptocurrency, uses the Proof of Work (PoW) consensus, where miners compete to solve complex mathematical puzzles, with the first to solve it receiving the right to add the next block to the blockchain. Other cryptocurrencies, like Ethereum, have explored alternative consensus mechanisms, such as Proof of Stake (PoS), where validators are selected to create new blocks based on the number of coins they "stake" as collateral.

The ever-expanding landscape of cryptocurrencies has not been without challenges. As the industry has grown, security, scalability, and energy consumption concerns have arisen. High-profile cryptocurrency exchange hacks, vulnerabilities in smart contracts, and debates over the environmental impact of energy-intensive mining processes have highlighted the need for continuous innovation and improvement in the space.

Despite these challenges, cryptocurrencies have garnered increasing attention from both individual and institutional investors. They offer a means of diversification, potential hedging against economic uncertainties, and access to emerging technological advancements. Moreover, cryptocurrencies have unlocked a new era of fundraising through Initial Coin Offerings (ICOs) and Security Token Offerings (STOs), allowing startups and projects to raise funds directly from global audiences.

As the understanding and adoption of cryptocurrencies continue to grow, regulators and policymakers worldwide have grappled with how to respond to this transformative technology. The regulatory landscape for cryptocurrencies varies widely from country to country, with some nations embracing innovation and promoting crypto-friendly environments, while others have taken a more cautious or restrictive approach.

In conclusion, cryptocurrencies represent a paradigm shift in the world of finance, with their decentralized, transparent, and secure nature challenging traditional financial systems. Understanding the definition of cryptocurrencies and the fundamental principles of blockchain technology is essential for anyone seeking to participate in this rapidly evolving space. As cryptocurrencies continue to evolve and influence various sectors, from finance to supply chain management, an informed understanding of their potential benefits, challenges, and risks becomes increasingly critical for individuals, businesses, policymakers, and researchers alike. The future of cryptocurrencies remains an exciting and transformative journey, with the potential to reshape the global financial landscape and empower individuals worldwide.

How cryptocurrencies work

Cryptocurrencies have captured the world's imagination, revolutionizing the way we perceive money and financial transactions. To comprehend the full potential and impact of cryptocurrencies, it is essential to understand how they work at their core. This section explores the underlying mechanisms of cryptocurrencies, delving into key concepts such as blockchain technology, cryptography, consensus mechanisms, and the process of creating and validating transactions.

Blockchain technology, a decentralized, unchangeable database that logs every transaction made through a network of computers, is the foundation of cryptocurrencies. Every transaction is compiled into a block, and these blocks are connected cryptographically to one another to create a chain of blocks. The whole transaction history is guaranteed to be clear, traceable, and impenetrable due to this design. The distributed nature of blockchain technology, in which multiple nodes throughout the network keep copies of the ledger, is one of its main features. Because there is no longer a requirement for a central authority, the system is more resilient to single points of failure and less vulnerable to hostile attacks.

The operation of cryptocurrencies depends heavily on cryptography. A set of cryptographic keys—the public and private keys—are produced via public-key cryptography. The public key is freely distributed and acts as an address to receive funds, as the name would imply. Conversely, the private key is used to sign transactions, proving ownership and approving fund transfers from the linked address. It is kept secret. Cryptographic keys ensure that only the owner of the private key has control over the cryptocurrency assets, providing security and privacy to users.

Cryptocurrencies employ various consensus mechanisms to achieve agreement on the state of the blockchain in a decentralized network. One of the earliest and most well-known mechanisms is Proof of Work (PoW), used by Bitcoin. The goal of Proof of Work (PoW) is for miners to compete by solving challenging mathematical puzzles; the first person to do so gets to add the succeeding block to the blockchain. This technique is energy-intensive but secure because it needs a lot of computing power. Ethereum and other cryptocurrencies use Proof of Stake (PoS), an alternative consensus technique. According to how many coins they "stake" as collateral, validators in proof of stake (PoS) are selected to create new blocks. PoS uses less energy than PoW, but in order to become validators, participants must own a sizable portion of the cryptocurrency.

The process of creating and validating transactions in cryptocurrencies is peer-to-peer and occurs without the need for intermediaries like banks. A transaction that a user initiates is broadcast to the network and assembled into a block together with other pending transactions. Competitors compete to verify the block of transactions and add it to the blockchain in the case of PoW (miners) or PoS (validators). To validate the block, they must solve a cryptographic puzzle or provide proof of their stake, depending on the consensus mechanism. Once the block is added to the blockchain, the transaction is confirmed and becomes a permanent public ledger.

In PoW-based cryptocurrencies, mining is an essential operation that entails resolving challenging mathematical puzzles in order to verify transactions and append new blocks to the blockchain. The first miner to solve the problem correctly wins newly created coins and transaction fees from the transactions in the block. Miners compete with one another to find the solution. Miners are encouraged to commit their processing power to securing the network and preserving the blockchain's integrity through this payment. Over time, the mining process becomes progressively more difficult, adjusting the difficulty level to maintain a consistent block generation rate.

The decentralized nature of cryptocurrencies lowers the possibility of a single point of failure or control, making it one of their primary advantages. Traditional financial systems are vulnerable to centralized attacks, but cryptocurrencies' distributed network makes them more resistant to malicious actors. Additionally, using cryptographic keys ensures that transactions are secure and private, as only the private key owner can access and transfer funds.

Beyond simple peer-to-peer transactions, some cryptocurrencies, like Ethereum, introduced the concept of smart contracts. Smart contracts are automatically carrying out agreements that have the terms of the contract encoded directly into the code. When certain circumstances are satisfied, they automatically run, doing away with the need for middlemen and lowering the likelihood of fraud or human error. Smart contracts open up a world of possibilities, enabling complex financial arrangements, supply chain management, and decentralized applications (DApps) to operate autonomously and transparently on the blockchain.

While many cryptocurrencies offer pseudonymous transactions, some have been specifically designed to prioritize user privacy and anonymity. Privacy coins, such as Monero and Zcash, implement advanced cryptographic techniques to obfuscate transaction details, making it challenging to trace the sender, recipient, or amount involved in a transaction. These privacy-focused cryptocurrencies cater to users who value their financial privacy and seek additional layers of security.

As cryptocurrencies gain popularity, scalability has become a critical concern. Traditional blockchains face challenges in processing many transactions quickly and efficiently. To address this, various scaling solutions have been proposed and implemented. Some projects, like Bitcoin's Lightning Network and Ethereum's Layer 2 solutions, aim to facilitate off-chain transactions to reduce congestion and increase throughput. Additionally, ongoing research and development in areas like sharding and state channels seek to optimize blockchain performance and accommodate the growing demand for decentralized applications.

The disruptive nature of cryptocurrencies has led to a patchwork of regulations globally. Some countries have embraced cryptocurrencies, providing a conducive environment for innovation and development, while others have imposed strict regulations to address fraud, money laundering, and consumer protection concerns. Achieving widespread adoption of cryptocurrencies requires balancing regulation and fostering innovation.

In conclusion, understanding how cryptocurrencies work is essential for anyone seeking to navigate the ever-changing landscape of digital currencies. From blockchain technology and consensus mechanisms to the process of creating and validating transactions, the fundamentals of cryptocurrencies underpin their transformative potential. The decentralized and secure nature of cryptocurrencies, coupled with innovative concepts like smart contracts, promises to reshape the financial and technological landscape. As cryptocurrencies evolve and gain broader acceptance, a comprehensive understanding of their mechanisms becomes increasingly vital for individuals, businesses, policymakers, and researchers. Harnessing the transformative power of cryptocurrencies necessitates staying informed and embracing the endless possibilities they present.

Blockchain technology and its significance

Blockchain technology, often hailed as one of the most disruptive innovations of the 21st century, has revolutionized industries and transformed how we envision trust, security, and data management. This section explores the essence of blockchain technology, its underlying principles, and its far-reaching significance in various domains, ranging from finance and supply chain management to healthcare and beyond. Understanding blockchain's fundamental concepts is essential for grasping its transformative potential and role in shaping decentralized systems' future.

A blockchain is fundamentally an immutable, distributed ledger that keeps track of transactions in a block-by-block order. A chain that guarantees the transparency and immutability of the complete transaction history is formed by each block, which consists of a list of transactions and a reference to the block before it. Blockchains are characterized by decentralization, in which copies of the ledger are dispersed throughout a network of computers called nodes. This distributed nature eliminates the need for a central authority, making blockchains resilient to single points of failure and resistant to censorship or unauthorized changes.

To maintain the integrity of the blockchain, blocks need to be added to the chain in a secure and verifiable manner. The process of adding blocks to the blockchain is called "mining" in Proof of Work (PoW) based blockchains. Miners compete to solve complicated mathematical puzzles, with the first to find the correct solution gaining the right to add the next block to the chain. The mining process requires significant computational power and energy, ensuring the network's security. Once a block is added, it becomes a permanent part of the blockchain, and altering any information in a block would require changing all subsequent blocks, making it practically infeasible.

Cryptography is a fundamental building block of blockchain technology, providing security and privacy to the network. Public-key cryptography generates a pair of cryptographic keys: public and private keys. The public key, visible to all, serves as an address for receiving transactions, while the private key is kept secret and used to sign transactions for spending funds. Cryptographic keys ensure that only the owner of the private key can control and authorize transactions associated with a particular address. Additionally, cryptographic hash functions are employed to link each block to the previous one, ensuring the immutability and integrity of the entire blockchain.

Blockchain's transparency and traceability are significant advantages for supply chain management. Stakeholders can gain real-time insights into the supply chain by recording each step of a product's journey on the blockchain, from raw materials to manufacturing, distribution, and retail. This transparency fosters trust among consumers and reduces the risk of counterfeit goods, as the origin and authenticity of products can be easily verified. For industries like food and pharmaceuticals, blockchain can improve safety by enabling swift and accurate recalls, thus preventing potential health hazards.

The implementation of smart contracts is one of the most potent uses of blockchain technology. Smart contracts are automatically carrying out agreements that have the terms of the contract encoded directly into the code. When certain circumstances are satisfied, they automatically run, doing away with the need for middlemen and lowering the likelihood of fraud or human error. Smart contracts open up a world of possibilities for various sectors, such as finance, insurance, real estate, and logistics. They can facilitate automated payments, conditional transactions, and decentralized applications, known as DApps, that operate transparently and autonomously.

Blockchain technology has the ability to bring financial inclusion to billions of people worldwide who are underserved by traditional banking systems. With a smartphone and internet connection, individuals can access blockchain-based financial services, such as digital wallets, remittances, and peer-to-peer lending. These services bypass the need for traditional intermediaries, making transactions more accessible, affordable, and efficient, particularly in regions with limited banking infrastructure.

Decentralized Finance, or DeFi, is a fast-growing sector within the blockchain space that aims to revolutionize traditional financial services. DeFi platforms offer various financial products and services, such as lending, borrowing, yield farming, and decentralized exchanges, all governed by smart contracts. DeFi removes the need for traditional financial intermediaries, making financial services more accessible and open to anyone with an internet connection. However, DeFi also comes with challenges like smart contract vulnerabilities and regulatory considerations.

While blockchain technology has demonstrated significant potential, challenges remain concerning interoperability and scalability. Interoperability is the ability of different blockchains to communicate and interact with each other seamlessly. Scalability, however, addresses the need for blockchains to handle many transactions quickly and efficiently. Addressing these challenges is essential for broader adoption of blockchain technology and ensuring that it can handle the demands of a global-scale network.

While blockchain technology offers robust security through cryptography and decentralization, it also presents unique data privacy challenges. Public blockchains, where transaction details are visible to all, may not be suitable for storing sensitive data. Privacy-focused blockchains, known as permissioned blockchains, address these concerns by restricting access to authorized participants. However, achieving a balance between transparency and data privacy remains an ongoing area of research and development.

As blockchain technology continues to gain traction, governments and regulatory bodies grapple with how to approach this disruptive technology. While some countries embrace blockchain innovation and provide a conducive environment for development, others impose stringent regulations to address fraud, money laundering, and consumer protection concerns. Balancing fostering innovation and safeguarding against potential risks is crucial for the responsible development and adoption of blockchain technology.

In conclusion, blockchain technology is a transformative force with far-reaching implications for various industries. Its decentralized and transparent nature revolutionizes trust, security, and data management, providing opportunities for financial inclusion, streamlined supply chains, and more efficient services. While challenges like scalability, interoperability, and data privacy persist, the potential of blockchain to reshape the world's systems and empower individuals and organizations alike remains undeniable. Embracing and understanding the significance of blockchain technology is vital for shaping its responsible development and harnessing its transformative potential for a more decentralized, efficient, and secure future.

Comparison with traditional currencies

The emergence of cryptocurrencies has sparked a profound shift in the financial landscape, prompting comparisons with traditional fiat currencies. At its core, cryptocurrencies are decentralized digital assets created through cryptographic principles, while traditional currencies, such as the US Dollar or Euro, are issued and regulated by central banks and governments. The decentralized nature of cryptocurrencies allows for a transparent and tamper-resistant ledger known as the blockchain, which is absent in traditional banking systems. While traditional currencies enjoy widespread acceptance as legal tender within their respective countries, cryptocurrencies face a diverse regulatory landscape, with some nations embracing them as legal assets or even legal tender, while others adopt a cautious approach with varying degrees of regulation or outright bans.

Transaction processing also sets cryptocurrencies apart from traditional currencies. Traditional banking systems often involve intermediaries like banks and financial institutions, leading to delays and additional fees in international transactions. In contrast, cryptocurrencies enable peer-to-peer transactions across borders with relatively faster processing times, thanks to the use of blockchain technology. This technology ensures the transparency and traceability of transactions, making verifying the authenticity of transfers on the public ledger easier. However, while the transaction details are transparent, the parties' identity can remain pseudonymous, providing a degree of privacy.

The issuance mechanisms of cryptocurrencies and traditional currencies also differ significantly. Traditional currencies are subject to centralized control by governments and central banks, allowing them to influence the money supply, interest rates, and implement monetary policies. In contrast, cryptocurrencies are created through predetermined algorithms, with some, like Bitcoin, having fixed supply caps, making them deflationary and resistant to inflationary pressures. This limited supply has contributed to the perception of cryptocurrencies as a store of value and a hedge against economic uncertainties.

One of the main advantages of cryptocurrencies lies in their potential to address financial inclusion challenges. With only an internet connection, individuals can access cryptocurrencies and engage in peer-to-peer transactions, remittances, and lending, regardless of their location or proximity to brick-and-mortar banks. While widely accepted, traditional currencies may not be accessible to individuals in remote or underserved regions with limited banking infrastructure.

Cryptocurrencies are also known for their price volatility, with values subject to significant fluctuations over short periods. Market sentiment, investor speculation, and technological developments can cause dramatic price swings in the cryptocurrency market. In contrast, traditional currencies, particularly those issued by stable and well-managed economies, tend to be more stable in value. Central banks implement monetary policies to maintain price stability and manage inflation, aiming to provide certainty and predictability to users and businesses.

While cryptocurrencies offer robust security through cryptographic protocols and decentralization, traditional currencies have also implemented security features to mitigate counterfeiting risks. Paper currencies, for example, may incorporate holograms, watermarks, and other specialized security features to safeguard against counterfeit attempts.

The environmental effect of cryptocurrencies has become a topic of concern, particularly for PoW-based blockchains like Bitcoin. Mining is the procedure of verifying transactions and adding blocks to the blockchain, requires substantial computational power, consuming significant amounts of electricity. Critics argue that the energy-intensive nature of mining contributes to carbon emissions and environmental degradation. On the other hand, traditional banking systems, while also energy-intensive, do not face the same level of scrutiny for their environmental impact.

As blockchain technology and the adoption of cryptocurrencies continue to evolve, central banks and governments have started to explore the development of Central Bank Digital Currencies (CBDCs). These are digital coins that are issued and managed by the central bank of a nation. Unlike cryptocurrencies, CBDCs would maintain a centralized issuance authority and be subject to traditional monetary policies. The introduction of CBDCs aims to enhance payment systems, promote financial inclusion, and improve the efficiency of monetary policies.

In conclusion, comparing cryptocurrencies and traditional currencies underscores the transformative potential of decentralized systems and blockchain technology. While traditional currencies play a crucial role in the global economy, cryptocurrencies offer innovative solutions, such as faster and more accessible cross-border transactions, decentralized financial services, and opportunities for financial inclusion. The coexistence of these two forms of currency shapes the future of finance, commerce, and global economic dynamics, prompting discussions around regulatory frameworks, security, and the broader implications on the financial landscape. Understanding these differences is vital for embracing the potential of cryptocurrencies and navigating the evolving financial ecosystem with awareness and informed decision-making.

CHAPTER III

Types of Cryptocurrencies

Bitcoin - The first and most popular cryptocurrency

The emergence of Bitcoin in 2009 marked a revolutionary milestone in finance and technology. Created by an anonymous entity or group operating under the pseudonym Satoshi Nakamoto, Bitcoin introduced the concept of a decentralized digital currency powered by blockchain technology. Whitepaper headlined "Bitcoin: A Peer-to-Peer Electronic Cash System" presented an explanation of how to tackle the persistent problem of double-spending in digital transactions. In order to do away with the necessity for a central authority, the plan was to establish a peer-to-peer network in which transactions are confirmed and documented by a consensus of network users on a public ledger, or blockchain.

The decentralized and unchangeable blockchain technology, which tracks every transaction made through a network of computers, is the fundamental component of what makes Bitcoin so revolutionary. Every transaction is compiled into a block, and these blocks are connected cryptographically to one another to create a chain of blocks. Because the blockchain is dispersed among a network of nodes, tamper-resistance, traceability, and transparency are guaranteed. This decentralized structure removes the need for intermediaries like banks and financial institutions, providing a direct and secure way for users to transact with each other.

One of the core tenets of Bitcoin is its decentralization and security. By operating on a peer-to-peer network, Bitcoin empowers individuals with financial sovereignty, allowing them to control their wealth without reliance on traditional banking systems. Transactions are secured through cryptographic protocols, making it highly resistant to fraud and counterfeiting. Mining is the process of approving and appending transactions to the blockchain. The first miner to correctly solve a challenging mathematical puzzle wins the right to add the next block to the chain. For mining to maintain network security, a large amount of computational power and energy are needed.

Bitcoin's monetary policy is distinct from traditional fiat currencies, which are subject to inflationary pressures. Bitcoin has a capped supply, with 21 million coins that will ever be created. As more coins are mined, the rate of new coin creation decreases over time, resulting in a deflationary effect. This limited supply has contributed to Bitcoin's reputation as a store of value and a potential hedge against economic uncertainties.

However, Bitcoin's price volatility has been a subject of both fascination and concern. Values experience dramatic fluctuations over short periods, driven by market sentiment, investor speculation, macroeconomic factors, and regulatory developments. The cryptocurrency market's relatively nascent state and the absence of regulatory clarity contribute to these price swings, creating both opportunities and risks for investors.

Despite its volatile nature, Bitcoin has garnered significant mainstream adoption over the years. Major companies, including Tesla and PayPal, have integrated Bitcoin into their business models, accepting it as a means of payment for goods and services. Institutional investors have also shown interest, with some adding Bitcoin to their investment portfolios as a diversification strategy.

However, Bitcoin has its challenges. One of the primary concerns is scalability. As the number of network transactions increases, the processing capacity of the blockchain can become constrained, leading to slower transaction period and higher fees. Several solutions, such as the Lightning Network, have been proposed to solve these challenges and improve scalability.

Bitcoin's popularity has also drawn attention from governments and regulatory bodies. The global regulatory landscape for cryptocurrencies is diverse and evolving, with some countries embracing cryptocurrencies and others taking a cautious approach. Regulatory clarity is crucial for the broader adoption and integration of Bitcoin into traditional financial systems.

Bitcoin's impact extends beyond its role as a digital currency. Its emergence has sparked discussions about the future of finance, the role of central banks, and the potential for a digital currency revolution. As central banks explore the development of Central Bank Digital Currencies (CBDCs) and businesses explore blockchain technology for various applications, the global financial landscape continues to experience significant disruption.

In conclusion, Bitcoin is the first and most popular cryptocurrency, representing a transformative force in the financial and technological realms. Its decentralized nature, secure blockchain technology, and limited supply have captured the imagination of individuals and institutions worldwide. As Bitcoin continues to evolve and gain broader acceptance, it remains at the forefront of the cryptocurrency movement, stimulating discussions about the future of finance, economic sovereignty, and the potential for decentralized systems to revolutionize the global economy. Understanding Bitcoin's genesis, underlying principles, and impact on the financial landscape is crucial for comprehending the broader implications of decentralized digital currencies and their potential to reshape the future of finance.

Altcoins - Overview of alternative cryptocurrencies

The rise of Bitcoin marked the beginning of a new era in the finance world, inspiring many alternative cryptocurrencies, commonly known as altcoins. Altcoins represent a diverse array of digital assets; each designed to address specific shortcomings of Bitcoin or cater to niche use cases. They have become essential to the cryptocurrency ecosystem, fostering innovation, competition, and diversification. Altcoins come in various forms, serving distinct purposes. Some prioritize user privacy, employing advanced cryptographic techniques to obfuscate transaction details, while others act as platforms for executing smart contracts, enabling decentralized applications and fostering the rise of decentralized finance (DeFi). Stablecoins offer price stability, utility tokens provide access to specific blockchain platforms, and exchange tokens offer benefits within cryptocurrency exchanges.

The creation of altcoins is driven by the desire to address limitations in existing cryptocurrencies and introduce novel features. Bitcoin's scalability, transaction speed, and privacy features have been subjects of criticism, prompting the development of altcoins with alternative consensus mechanisms and privacy protocols. By fostering innovation, altcoins have served as catalysts for the growth of the broader cryptocurrency ecosystem. Smart contract platforms, exemplified by Ethereum, have enabled the creation of various decentralized applications, while privacy coins have offered users enhanced privacy and anonymity in transactions.

However, altcoins have challenges and risks. Many altcoins experience higher levels of price volatility than Bitcoin, which can be attributed to market sentiment and speculation. Liquidity and adoption can also be issues for certain altcoins, limiting their tradability and real-world use cases. Moreover, security vulnerabilities and regulatory uncertainty pose risks to altcoin projects, requiring diligent measures by their development communities and navigating through evolving regulatory landscapes.

The success and relevance of altcoin projects depend on various factors, including technological robustness, clear use cases, adoption by users and businesses, and a vibrant development community. Ethereum's success as a smart contract platform illustrates the transformative potential of well-executed altcoin projects, revolutionizing various sectors through DeFi, NFTs, and beyond. However, there have also been altcoin projects that have faced difficulties or controversies, highlighting the importance of substance and credibility in cryptocurrency.

Looking ahead, altcoins are expected to coexist with Bitcoin and other cryptocurrencies, offering unique value propositions and catering to particular needs in the market. They will continue to drive innovation and competition, contributing to the growth and maturation of the cryptocurrency ecosystem. As the cryptocurrency space evolves, altcoins will remain essential in shaping the future of finance, decentralization, and blockchain technology.

In conclusion, altcoins represent a diverse and innovative segment of the cryptocurrency landscape. They have emerged as alternatives to Bitcoin, providing solutions to specific challenges and facilitating the growth of decentralized finance and other applications. The various categories of altcoins, such as privacy coins, smart contract platforms, stablecoins, utility tokens, and exchange tokens, cater to different use cases, offering diverse possibilities for users and investors. While altcoins face challenges and uncertainties, their presence drives innovation, fosters competition, and builds a vibrant cryptocurrency ecosystem. As they continue to evolve and coexist with Bitcoin and other cryptocurrencies, altcoins will undoubtedly play a significant role in shaping the future of finance and technology.

Stablecoins - Cryptocurrencies with stable value

The cryptocurrency market is notorious for its price volatility, and while this volatility can be appealing for traders and speculators, it presents challenges for everyday use and mainstream adoption. Enter stablecoins, a unique subset of cryptocurrencies designed to provide stability in a realm characterized by price fluctuations. Stablecoins seek to provide the best of both worlds - the efficiency and borderless nature of cryptocurrencies combined with the stability of traditional fiat currencies. They achieve this by pegging their value to a stable asset, like a fiat currency or a commodity, ensuring a 1:1 value ratio.

Stablecoins are required because there is a demand for the creation of a trustworthy unit of account, an effective means of exchange, and a store of value that can be utilized for day-to-day financial activities as well as other types of transactions. While revolutionary in their concepts, Bitcoin and other cryptocurrencies are hindered by their price volatility, making them less practical for everyday use. Stablecoins address this issue by maintaining a stable value, making them more suitable for daily financial interactions.

Stablecoins employ various mechanisms to maintain their price stability. Some stablecoins are supported by a fiat currency reserve or other assets held in custodial accounts. For example, a stablecoin pegged to the US Dollar would have an equivalent amount of USD held in reserve for every stablecoin issued. Other stablecoins utilize algorithms to dynamically adjust the supply based on market conditions, ensuring the stablecoin's value remains consistent.

Stablecoins can be categorized based on their underlying mechanisms and the type of asset they are pegged to. The three main categories are fiat-collateralized, crypto-collateralized, and algorithmic stablecoins. Users of fiat-collateralized stablecoins can feel secure in the knowledge that they are supported by a reserve of fiat currency. Examples include Tether (USDT), USD Coin (USDC), and TrueUSD (TUSD). Crypto-collateralized stablecoins, on the other hand, use other cryptocurrencies as collateral. Users lock up a certain amount of cryptocurrency, and stablecoins are issued against it. Examples of crypto-collateralized stablecoins include DAI, which is collateralized by Ethereum, and sUSD, collateralized by Synthetix Network Token (SNX). Finally, algorithmic stablecoins rely on complex algorithms to adjust supply and demand dynamically, maintaining the stablecoin's value. Examples include Ampleforth (AMPL) and Terra (LUNA).

Stablecoins have found numerous applications within the cryptocurrency space and beyond. They are particularly well-suited for remittances and cross-border payments, offering a faster and more cost-effective alternative to traditional payment systems. Stablecoins also play a central role in decentralized finance (DeFi) platforms, providing a stable unit of account for borrowing, lending, and yield farming activities. Furthermore, stablecoins enable tokenizing real-world assets, making illiquid assets more accessible to investors. Investors also use stablecoins as a hedge against market volatility, protecting their wealth during times of uncertainty.

While stablecoins offer unique advantages, they also face challenges and risks. Some fiat-collateralized stablecoins rely on centralized custodians to hold the reserve assets, introducing counterparty risk and concerns about transparency and security. Additionally, regulatory scrutiny has increased as stablecoins, especially those pegged to fiat currencies, have gained popularity. Questions about classification, reserve requirements, and potential impact on monetary policy have sparked discussions in regulatory circles. Crypto-collateralized stablecoins are susceptible to smart contract vulnerabilities, and algorithmic stablecoins rely on complex mechanisms that may lead to unexpected outcomes.

Despite the challenges, stablecoins have cemented their position as an essential element within the cryptocurrency ecosystem. As the world moves toward a digital economy, stablecoins are expected to play an increasingly significant role in various financial transactions and interactions. Their ability to combine the advantages of cryptocurrencies with price stability has attracted interest from individuals, businesses, and institutional players alike.

In conclusion, stablecoins represent a critical bridge between the volatile world of cryptocurrencies and the stable realm of traditional finance. By offering stability and predictability, stablecoins address a significant concern that has hindered mainstream adoption of digital assets. With their diverse categories, including fiat-collateralized, crypto-collateralized, and algorithmic stablecoins, they cater to various needs and preferences. Stablecoins have found applications in remittances, DeFi, tokenization, and wealth preservation. As they continue to evolve and regulatory frameworks mature, stablecoins have the potential to become a fundamental component of the global financial system, transforming the way we transact and manage value in the digital age.

Utility tokens and security tokens

The cryptocurrency ecosystem has seen a proliferation of various digital assets, each serving different purposes and offering unique features. Among the wide array of tokens, two prominent categories are utility tokens and security tokens. These tokens play essential roles in blockchain technology and digital finance, but they are fundamentally distinct in their design, use cases, and regulatory implications.

Utility tokens are digital assets that permit users access to specific goods or services within a decentralized network or ecosystem. They are typically issued by blockchain projects to fuel their platforms and incentivize user engagement. Unlike traditional cryptocurrencies like Bitcoin, which serve as a means of value transfer, utility tokens have a distinct utility or function within a specific blockchain network. For instance, within a decentralized social media platform, a utility token might be used to tip content creators, access premium features, or participate in governance mechanisms.

On the other hand, security tokens represent digital ownership of traditional assets, such as equities, bonds, real estate, or investment funds. Unlike utility tokens, which derive their value from their utility within a specific ecosystem, security tokens derive their value from the underlying asset or financial instrument. Security tokens are issued and regulated in compliance with securities laws and regulations, subjecting them to stringent legal requirements.

The primary distinctions between utility and security tokens lie in purpose, value proposition, and regulatory treatment. Utility tokens are designed to offer access to goods or services within a specific decentralized ecosystem, incentivizing user engagement and promoting network effects. Security tokens, conversely, represent ownership or investment in real-world assets or financial instruments.

The regulatory landscape for utility tokens and security tokens is complex and continually evolving. Regulators worldwide are grappling with the unique characteristics of digital assets and seeking to apply existing securities laws and regulations to this new paradigm. The classification of tokens may change based on regulatory interpretations and jurisdiction.

Despite the regulatory challenges, utility and security tokens hold immense potential for reshaping traditional finance and democratizing access to assets and investment opportunities. Utility tokens play a crucial role in incentivizing user participation and promoting the growth of decentralized networks. They enable novel business models and reward mechanisms, encouraging innovative use cases in content creation, gaming, and social media sectors.

On the other hand, security tokens offer a pathway to digitize and tokenize traditional assets, unlocking liquidity and accessibility for a broader range of investors. Fractional ownership and global market access reduce barriers to entry, making traditionally illiquid assets more liquid and tradable.

In conclusion, utility tokens and security tokens represent two distinct yet interconnected facets of the tokenization revolution. Utility tokens empower decentralized ecosystems, driving engagement and network growth through incentivization mechanisms. On the other hand, security tokens digitize traditional assets and financial instruments, offering increased liquidity and accessibility to global investors.

The potential of tokenization lies in its ability to reshape traditional finance, create new opportunities for global investors, and democratize access to investment opportunities. As the regulatory landscape continues to evolve, finding a balance between innovation and investor protection will be crucial in unlocking utility and security tokens' full potential in the cryptocurrency ecosystem. As the technology matures, tokenization can revolutionize traditional finance, democratize access to assets, and reshape the global economy for the better.

CHAPTER IV

Getting Started with Cryptocurrencies

Setting up a cryptocurrency wallet

In the rapidly evolving world of cryptocurrencies, owning and managing a cryptocurrency wallet is essential for anyone seeking to participate in this decentralized financial landscape. A cryptocurrency wallet is a digital tool allowing users to keep, send, and receive digital assets securely. Unlike traditional wallets holding physical cash and cards, cryptocurrency wallets keep private keys, essential for accessing and managing your digital assets on the blockchain. This section explores the various types of cryptocurrency wallets, the step-by-step process of setting up a wallet, security considerations, and best practices for safeguarding your valuable digital assets.

Cryptocurrency wallets can be broadly categorized into four main types: hardware wallets, software wallets, paper wallets, and online wallets. Hardware wallets are tangible devices specifically designed to store private keys offline, offering the highest level of security as they keep the private keys isolated from internet-connected devices. On the other hand, software wallets are applications that can be installed on smartphones, computers, or other devices. They come in various forms, such as desktop wallets, mobile wallets, and web wallets, each offering different levels of security and convenience. Paper wallets involve printing the private keys on paper, providing offline storage for enhanced security. Online wallets, or web wallets or custodial wallets, are offered by cryptocurrency exchanges and other third-party platforms, but they store users' private keys on their servers, making them less secure compared to other types of wallets.

Setting up a cryptocurrency wallet can vary depending on the type of wallet you choose. For a software wallet, which is one of the most commonly used wallet types, the steps include choosing a wallet, downloading and installing the official application from a reputable source, creating a new wallet with a strong password, and backing up the wallet's recovery phrase or seed phrase. The recovery phrase is a sequence of words that can be used to restore access to the wallet in case of device loss, damage, or theft. It's crucial to securely store the recovery phrase offline in multiple physical locations to prevent potential loss.

Security considerations are of utmost importance when it comes to managing a cryptocurrency wallet. Keeping your private keys secure is paramount, and they should be treated with the same level of care and protection as your physical keys or passwords. Enabling two-factor authentication (2FA) whenever possible adds an extra layer of security to your wallet. Being cautious of phishing attempts and avoiding sharing your private keys or recovery phrase with anyone are critical to safeguarding your digital assets. Regularly updating your wallet software and considering cold storage options, like hardware or paper wallets, for large amounts of cryptocurrency are additional measures to enhance security.

To ensure the long-term security of your cryptocurrency wallet, follow best practices for wallet management, including regular backups of the recovery phrase, testing small transactions before sending significant amounts, staying informed about the latest security practices and trends, and diversifying your holdings across multiple wallets. By adhering to these practices and keeping yourself updated on potential threats and vulnerabilities, you can confidently safeguard your digital assets and participate responsibly in the decentralized financial landscape. As cryptocurrency evolves, protecting your wallet and assets will remain fundamental to being a responsible and secure participant in this revolutionary financial ecosystem.

Understanding public and private keys

In the world of cryptography and digital assets, public and private keys are fundamental components that form the backbone of secure communication, authentication, and ownership verification. These cryptographic keys play a pivotal role in the functioning of cryptocurrencies, ensuring secure transactions and enabling users to maintain control over their digital assets.

Public keys are cryptographic keys that are openly shared and visible to all users within the network. They are used to generate wallet addresses, serving as a user's public identity on the blockchain. Users who want to receive funds or cryptocurrency share their wallet address or public key with the sender. The sender then uses this public key to encrypt the transaction data, ensuring that only the intended recipient can decrypt and access the funds. Since the public key is visible to everyone, it can be freely distributed across the network, enabling secure communication and transactions without revealing the user's private key.

In contrast, private keys are confidential and secret cryptographic keys known only to the user. They grant ownership and control over digital assets and are derived from a random seed or a combination of unique factors. With the private key, users can sign transactions, proving their ownership of specific digital assets and authorizing their transfer to another user's wallet address. Since the private key must remain confidential, users must safeguard it from unauthorized access, loss, or theft. Losing access to the private key can permanently lose the associated digital assets, as there is no centralized authority to recover or reset it.

The relationship between public and private keys lies at the heart of asymmetric cryptography, also known as public-key cryptography. Asymmetric cryptography relies on a pair of keys - one public and one private - that are mathematically related but computationally infeasible to reverse-engineer. Any data encrypted with a user's public key can only be decrypted using their corresponding private key and vice versa. This ensures secure communication and verification without requiring users to exchange their private keys directly.

Public and private keys are central to securing cryptocurrency transactions on the blockchain. When users initiate a transaction, they use their private key to make a digital signature that uniquely identifies them as the sender. This signature is appended to the transaction data and the recipient's public key or wallet address. The transaction, along with the digital signature, is then broadcast to the network and validated by the consensus mechanism employed by the blockchain. The network confirms the digital signature using the sender's public key to ensure the transaction's authenticity and that it has not been tampered with. If the verification is successful, the transaction is added to a block and added to the blockchain, completing the transfer of digital assets.

The security of public and private keys is paramount in cryptocurrencies. Since private keys grant ownership and control over digital assets, they are a main target for hackers and malicious actors. Generating strong keys, using hardware wallets for added security, and enabling two-factor authentication are essential practices to safeguard cryptographic keys. Regularly backing up private keys and being cautious of phishing attempts are critical to protecting digital assets from loss or theft.

Beyond cryptocurrencies, public and private keys have applications in various digital security scenarios. They are integral to secure communication protocols like Transport Layer Security (TLS) and Pretty Good Privacy (PGP), ensuring encrypted data transmission and email encryption with digital signatures. Their robustness and mathematical properties make them crucial for safeguarding sensitive information and upholding digital privacy in various industries and applications.

In conclusion, public and private keys are the bedrock of cryptographic security in cryptocurrencies and digital communication. Public keys enable secure transactions and communication, while private keys grant ownership and control over digital assets. Based on asymmetric cryptography, the relationship between public and private keys ensures secure communication and authentication without the need for direct key exchange. Anyone working with cryptocurrencies and digital security needs to be aware of these concepts since they are critical to safeguarding transactions and shielding digital assets from malevolent assaults and unlawful access. Public and private keys will continue to be essential for guaranteeing private and safe interactions in the digital age as the digital landscape develops.

Choosing a reliable cryptocurrency exchange

The need for trustworthy cryptocurrency exchanges has increased dramatically as the use of cryptocurrencies continues to gain traction. Cryptocurrency exchanges are the gateways for buying, selling, and trading digital assets, making them critical platforms for investors and traders. However, the increasing number of exchanges and the risk of scams and security breaches highlight the importance of choosing a reliable cryptocurrency exchange.

One of the first aspects to consider when choosing a cryptocurrency exchange is its reputation and track record in the industry. Research the exchange's history, user reviews, and its standing in the cryptocurrency community. Look for exchanges that have been operational for a significant period and have a proven track record of reliable services and customer support. Established exchanges with positive feedback from users are more likely to be trustworthy and provide a better user experience.

Exchanges for cryptocurrencies must prioritize security. Look for platforms that implement robust security measures to safeguard user funds and data. Two-factor authentication (2FA) should be available to enhance account security. Additionally, the exchange should employ industry-standard encryption protocols to protect sensitive information. A reliable exchange will have transparent information about its security practices and may even conduct regular security audits by third-party firms to demonstrate its commitment to user safety.

Ensure that the cryptocurrency exchange you choose complies with relevant regulations in the jurisdictions where it operates. Regulatory compliance is essential for protecting user interests and ensuring the exchange adheres to financial and security standards. Licensed and regulated exchanges are more likely to prioritize customer protection and adhere to anti-money laundering (AML) and know-your-customer (KYC) requirements.

Consider the range of cryptocurrencies and trading pairs offered by the exchange. Different exchanges support different digital assets, and the availability of the cryptocurrencies you wish to trade is crucial. If you have specific altcoins in mind, ensure the exchange provides access to them. Moreover, check the liquidity of the trading pairs, as higher liquidity facilitates smoother trading experiences and better price execution.

The user interface and experience significantly influence your overall trading journey. Choose an exchange with an intuitive and user-friendly interface that caters to beginners and experienced traders. A cluttered or confusing platform can lead to costly mistakes, especially for new users. Look for exchanges with well-designed dashboards, clear navigation, and easy access to essential features.

Prompt and effective customer support is essential in the fast-paced cryptocurrency market. Look for exchanges that offer multiple customer support channels, which includes email, live chat, or phone support. A responsive support team can promptly address your concerns and resolve issues, ensuring a smoother trading experience. Examine the fee structure of the exchange before signing up. Different exchanges charge various fees for deposits, withdrawals, and trades. Some exchanges offer tiered fee structures based on trading volume, providing cost advantages for high-volume traders. Be aware of hidden fees or unusual charges, and compare the fee structures of different exchanges to make an informed decision.

Think about the payment options that the exchange accepts. Some exchanges allow fiat deposits and withdrawals, while others may only support cryptocurrency transfers. If you plan to buy cryptocurrencies with fiat money, be sure the exchange takes your preferred payment method, which includes credit cards or bank transfers.

In an era of mobile connectivity, accessing your cryptocurrency exchange on the go is advantageous. Look for exchanges that offer mobile apps compatible with your device's operating system. Mobile support allows you to monitor the market, execute trades, and manage your portfolio conveniently from your smartphone or tablet. Reliable exchanges may offer insurance coverage or employ fund protection mechanisms to safeguard user funds. Insurance against security breaches or cyberattacks can provide traders with an additional layer of confidence. Fund protection mechanisms, such as cold wallets for storing most user funds offline, demonstrate the exchange's commitment to security.

Before finalizing your decision, conduct thorough research and due diligence on the exchange. Seek information from reputable sources, read reviews from other users, and check for any negative feedback or red flags. Look for exchanges with a transparent and open communication policy, providing regular updates and promptly addressing user concerns.

Once you have chosen a reliable cryptocurrency exchange, following best practices to safeguard your digital assets is essential. Enable two-factor authentication (2FA) to add an extra layer of security to your exchange account. Consider using hardware wallets for long-term storage of significant amounts of cryptocurrencies. Hardware wallets protect your private keys from online attacks by keeping them offline. Maintain up-to-date security patches and upgrades on your devices and exchange account software by updating them on a regular basis. If the exchange gives you a recovery phrase, make sure you safely store it in several different places so you can access your account again in case something goes wrong. Steer clear of suspicious links and don't give private information to unidentified sources. Watch out for efforts to obtain your account credentials through phishing. Keep a regular eye out for any unusual activity or unwanted access to your account. If you see anything odd, get in touch with customer service right away. If you notice anything suspicious, contact customer support immediately.

In conclusion, choosing a reliable cryptocurrency exchange is crucial for safely navigating the dynamic and rapidly evolving cryptocurrency market. When evaluating an exchange, consider factors such as reputation, security measures, regulatory compliance, available cryptocurrencies, user interface, customer support, fees, payment methods, mobile support, insurance, and fund protection. Conduct an in-depth research and due diligence to ensure the exchange meets your requirements and security standards. Following best practices to safeguard your digital assets further enhances the security of your exchange account and digital holdings. By taking these precautions and selecting a reputable exchange, you can confidently engage in cryptocurrency trading, investment, and exploration, knowing that your assets are safe. As the cryptocurrency landscape evolves, staying informed about security best practices and keeping abreast of exchange developments will help you make informed decisions and protect your valuable digital assets in the ever-expanding world of cryptocurrencies.

Buying, selling, and trading cryptocurrencies

The world of cryptocurrencies has revolutionized the way we perceive and interact with money. Purchasing, selling, and trading digital assets have grown into essential components of this decentralized financial environment as the acceptance of cryptocurrencies continues to skyrocket. This section delves into the processes of buying, selling, and trading cryptocurrencies, exploring the different methods and platforms available, the risks and benefits, essential considerations for successful trading, and the evolving role of cryptocurrencies in the global financial ecosystem.

Purchasing cryptocurrencies is the first step for individuals seeking to enter the world of digital assets. Several methods to acquire cryptocurrencies cater to various preferences and needs. One of the most common methods is buying cryptocurrencies through cryptocurrency exchanges. These platforms enable users to exchange fiat currency, such as USD or EUR, for cryptocurrencies like Bitcoin, Ethereum, or Litecoin. The process entails creating an account on the exchange, completing the necessary identity verification (KYC) process, and funding the account using a preferred payment method. Once the funds are available, users can place buy orders at the desired cryptocurrency's current market price or set a specific price point at which they wish to purchase the asset.

In addition to exchanges, some peer-to-peer (P2P) platforms enable direct transactions between buyers and sellers. P2P platforms facilitate interactions without intermediaries, providing a decentralized and often more private approach to buying cryptocurrencies. These platforms allow users to browse available offers, negotiate prices, and execute transactions directly with other users.

Cryptocurrency ATMs are another option for purchasing digital assets, allowing users to buy cryptocurrencies using cash or credit/debit cards. These ATMs are located in various physical locations, providing convenience and accessibility to those without access to online exchanges.

Selling cryptocurrencies is the process of converting digital assets back into fiat currency or other cryptocurrencies. Much like buying, selling cryptocurrencies can be done through cryptocurrency exchanges or P2P platforms. To sell on an exchange, users typically follow a similar process as buying, but this time they create a sell order instead. They set the amount of cryptocurrency they wish to sell and either accept the current market price or set a specific price point at which they want to execute the sale.

P2P platforms also enable users to sell cryptocurrencies directly to interested buyers. Sellers can create listings with the amount of cryptocurrency they want to sell, the desired price, and payment methods they accept. Buyers can then browse through available listings and initiate transactions with the sellers of their choice.

Cryptocurrency ATMs may also offer the option to sell digital assets, allowing users to exchange their cryptocurrencies for cash or credit/debit card payments.

Trading cryptocurrencies is a more dynamic and speculative activity, involving buying and selling digital assets to profit from price fluctuations. Cryptocurrency trading can be conducted on various platforms, including cryptocurrency exchanges and specialized trading platforms.

There are two main trading strategies: long-term and short-term trading. Long-term trading, often referred to as "HODLing" (derived from "hold" misspelled), involves buying cryptocurrencies and holding them for an extended period, anticipating their value to increase over time. Long-term traders rely on fundamental analysis, assessing the project's potential behind the cryptocurrency and its adoption in the real world.

On the other hand, short-term trading, commonly known as day trading or swing trading, involves frequent purchasing and selling of cryptocurrencies within shorter timeframes, such as hours or days. Short-term traders utilize technical analysis, examining price charts, patterns, and market indicators to make quick and frequent trading decisions.

Both trading strategies carry inherent risks, and success in trading requires comprehensive research, knowledge of market trends, risk management skills, and a disciplined approach to decision-making. Traders should only invest funds they can afford to lose and be prepared for the volatile nature of the cryptocurrency market.

While buying, selling, and trading cryptocurrencies offer exciting opportunities, they also have inherent risks and benefits. Volatility is one of the main risks, with cryptocurrency values capable of experiencing significant swings in short periods, leading to substantial gains or losses for investors and traders. Security risks are also a concern, as holding cryptocurrencies on exchanges or online wallets poses security risks, with hackers and cybercriminals potentially targeting these platforms. Additionally, regulatory uncertainties, scams, and fraudulent schemes are challenges that investors and traders must navigate.

On the positive side, cryptocurrencies offer decentralization, allowing users greater authority over their funds and financial transactions. They are globally accessible, providing financial inclusion for individuals in unbanked or underbanked regions. The cryptocurrency market operates 24/7, offering flexibility and accessibility for traders worldwide. Including cryptocurrencies in an investment portfolio can serve as a diversification strategy, potentially reducing overall risk and enhancing potential returns. Furthermore, cryptocurrencies and blockchain technology present opportunities for innovation and transformative applications across various industries.

To succeed in cryptocurrency trading, individuals should educate themselves, manage risks effectively, stay informed on market trends, avoid emotional decisions, start with small investments to gain experience, and prioritize security measures to protect their funds. Moreover, as the role of cryptocurrencies continues to evolve, they are reshaping the financial landscape, prompting traditional financial institutions to explore blockchain technology, and leading governments and central banks to consider issuing their own central bank digital currencies (CBDCs).

In conclusion, buying, selling, and trading cryptocurrencies have become integral activities in the world of digital finance. Effectively navigating the cryptocurrency market necessitates thorough study, risk management, and a disciplined attitude, regardless of whether one is an active trader or long-term investor. The dynamic nature of the market, coupled with its potential for significant gains and losses, demands caution and prudence.

While the risks are real, so are the opportunities. Cryptocurrencies and blockchain technology offer transformative potential, reshaping the financial landscape and empowering individuals with greater control over their finances. Embracing the opportunities while mitigating the risks will help navigate the ever-evolving world of cryptocurrencies and contribute to the ongoing transformation of the global financial ecosystem. As the cryptocurrency market evolves, educating oneself, staying informed, and adopting responsible practices will position individuals to make informed decisions and harness the potential of this groundbreaking digital revolution.

CHAPTER V

Storing and Securing Cryptocurrencies

Hardware wallets

Cryptocurrencies have empowered individuals with more significant financial sovereignty and asset control. As digital currencies gain popularity, ensuring the security of these valuable digital holdings becomes paramount. Amidst the growing concerns of cyberattacks, scams, and online thefts, hardware wallets have emerged as a robust solution to safeguard cryptocurrencies. This section delves into the significance of hardware wallets, their functionalities, their advantages over other storage methods, key considerations for selecting the right hardware wallet, and best practices for maximizing security.

Hardware wallets are tangible devices designed to store private keys securely, the cryptographic keys that grant access to one's cryptocurrencies. Unlike software wallets (e.g., desktop or mobile wallets), which store private keys on internet-connected devices, hardware wallets keep the keys offline, providing an additional layer of security. The offline nature of hardware wallets reduces the risk of exposure to online threats, such as phishing attempts, malware, and hacking attacks. The private key is securely stored inside the hardware wallet and is used to sign transactions when a user initiates a cryptocurrency transaction. This ensures that the private key is never removed from the hardware wallet's safe and secure environment.

Hardware wallets offer several functionalities and features contributing to their appeal as a secure storage solution for cryptocurrencies. These features include secure private key generation, offline storage, encryption, backup and recovery options, multi-currency support, and a user-friendly interface.

While software wallets, online wallets, and exchange wallets provide convenient options for storing cryptocurrencies, they have certain vulnerabilities that hardware wallets effectively address. Hardware wallets offer enhanced security due to their offline storage and cryptographic protection, reducing the risk of hacks and cyberattacks. They protect against malware and phishing attempts that target software and online wallets. Additionally, hardware wallets give users full control and ownership of their private keys, eliminating reliance on third-party services.

Selecting the right hardware wallet is essential to ensure the security and ease of managing cryptocurrencies. Users should consider security features, supported cryptocurrencies, user interface, reputation, backup and recovery options, and physical durability when choosing a hardware wallet.

To maximize security, users should purchase hardware wallets from official sources, set strong PINs and passphrases, keep the recovery seed phrase offline and in multiple secure locations, regularly update firmware, avoid using public Wi-Fi, and be cautious of phishing attempts and scams.

In the dynamic landscape of cryptocurrencies, embracing hardware wallets as a fortified vault for your digital fortunes is a prudent step towards safeguarding your valuable assets. With hardware wallets at your disposal, you can confidently navigate the world of cryptocurrencies, knowing that your digital fortunes are well-protected and under your control. As technology advances and security measures improve, hardware wallets will be pivotal in empowering individuals with control over their financial destinies in the digital age.

Software wallets

The demand for safe and convenient storage options grows as cryptocurrencies continue to gain traction in the financial sector. Software wallets, also known as digital wallets or hot wallets, have emerged as a popular choice for storing and managing cryptocurrencies. These software-based solutions provide users convenient access to their digital assets, allowing them to send, receive, and monitor their holdings easily.

Software wallets are applications that store private keys, which are the cryptographic keys necessary to access and control one's cryptocurrencies. Unlike hardware wallets, which hold private keys on dedicated physical devices, software wallets are installed on internet-connected devices, such as desktop computers, laptops, tablets, or mobile phones. The key advantage of software wallets is their accessibility and ease of use. For those who regularly transact with cryptocurrencies, the wallet application is convenient since it can be downloaded and installed on their devices.

Software wallets come in various types, each catering to different user needs and preferences. Common types include desktop, mobile, online, and hardware-secured wallets. Desktop wallets are software applications installed on desktop computers or laptops, providing a more secure option as private keys are kept locally on the user's device. On the other hand, mobile wallets are apps designed for smartphones and tablets, offering portability and allowing users to manage cryptocurrencies on the go. Online wallets, or web wallets, are hosted on the cloud and accessed within a web browser, providing convenience but also making them more susceptible to security risks. Some software wallets can be combined with hardware security devices, such as USB dongles or smart cards, to enhance security.

Security is a critical aspect of storing cryptocurrencies in software wallets. While software wallets offer convenience, they are inherently more vulnerable to online threats than hardware wallets. Key security considerations include private key control, password protection, backup and recovery, regular updates, secure devices, multi-factor authentication, and phishing awareness. Users must control their private keys and set strong passwords to protect access to their wallets. Creating backups of private keys or seed phrases is essential for recovery in case of device loss or damage. Regularly updating the wallet software ensures the latest security patches are applied. Using dedicated and secure devices for managing cryptocurrencies can minimize the risk of exposure to malware or hacking attempts. Enabling multi-factor authentication adds a further layer of security, requiring additional verification before accessing funds. Users should be cautious of phishing attempts and only access wallets through official websites or trusted sources.

Software wallets offer several advantages, making them popular among cryptocurrency users. They are easy to set up and use, providing accessibility to users with varying technical expertise. Software wallets also offer convenience, allowing quick and seamless transactions on internet-connected devices. Many software wallets support multiple cryptocurrencies, enabling users to manage various digital assets within a single application. Mobile wallets provide the added benefit of managing cryptocurrencies on the go, enhancing user flexibility. However, software wallets also have limitations, including security risks due to their online nature. Users must trust third-party service providers with their private keys in the case of online wallets, which can be a risk if the service experiences a security breach. Additionally, losing access to private keys or forgetting passwords can permanently lose funds.

Users should follow best practices to maximize the security of cryptocurrencies stored in software wallets. Setting strong and unique passwords, creating multiple backups of private keys or seed phrases, regularly updating wallet software, using hardware wallets or offline storage for long-term holdings, enabling multi-factor authentication, being cautious of phishing attempts, and using dedicated and secure devices are essential steps. By adhering to these practices, users can fortify their digital fortunes and confidently navigate the world of cryptocurrencies with software wallets as their digital guardians. As technology evolves, software wallet developers will likely enhance security features, making them an increasingly reliable and secure cryptocurrency storage and management option.

Paper wallets

In the ever-expanding world of cryptocurrencies, security remains a top priority for investors and enthusiasts alike. As digital assets continue to gain popularity, individuals seek reliable and offline storage solutions to protect their valuable holdings from online threats. Paper wallets have emerged as a timeless and straightforward method for storing and securing cryptocurrencies.

Paper wallets represent a simplistic yet powerful approach to storing cryptocurrencies securely offline. A paper wallet is essentially a physical copy or printout of a cryptocurrency's public and private keys. The public key allows users to receive funds, while the private key grants access and control over those funds. Unlike software and hardware wallets that store private keys electronically, paper wallets maintain them physically, immune to online threats like hacking, malware, and phishing attacks.

Creating a paper wallet involves generating a pair of public and private keys and then recording them on a physical medium, typically a piece of paper. To create a paper wallet, users can use a reliable offline tool or a dedicated website that generates the keys securely. Some paper wallet generators even allow users to add additional layers of security, such as BIP38 encryption, which requires a passphrase to access the private key, providing an extra safeguard in case the physical wallet is compromised.

Paper wallets offer several distinct advantages, making them a popular choice for long-term cryptocurrency storage. First and foremost, paper wallets are entirely offline, eliminating the risk of online attacks and unauthorized access to private keys. Users control and store the keys themselves, retaining full ownership and control of their funds without relying on third-party services. This aligns with the decentralized ethos of cryptocurrencies, as paper wallets do not require intermediaries or internet connectivity to function. Paper wallets are well-suited for long-term storage, offering durability and resilience over extended periods.

Despite their benefits, paper wallets also come with certain limitations that users should be aware of. Paper wallets are physical documents susceptible to damage, loss, or theft. To mitigate these risks, users must store them securely and protect them from elements that could cause deterioration. Transactions with paper wallets are less convenient than digital wallets, as users must import or sweep the private key into a hardware or software wallet to access their funds. Lastly, paper wallets cannot be backed up electronically, necessitating the creation of multiple physical copies stored in secure locations.

Several key considerations can enhance security and ensure a smooth experience when generating and using paper wallets. Creating paper wallets on an offline computer is essential to minimize exposure to online threats. Users should also use a secure printer to avoid potential leakage of private key information during printing. Creating multiple copies of the paper wallet and storing them in secure, separate locations can guard against loss or damage. To protect paper wallets from environmental factors, users may consider laminating or encasing them.

Users should adhere to best practices to ensure the utmost security and safeguard the funds stored in paper wallets. Generating paper wallets on reputable and secure offline devices is crucial. Storing paper wallets in secure, fireproof, and waterproof locations, such as a safe or a bank safety deposit box, is essential to protect them from physical threats. Users must also regularly check for signs of tampering or unauthorized access to ensure the integrity of the paper wallet.

In conclusion, paper wallets offer a timeless and elegant method for storing and securing cryptocurrencies offline. The simplicity and user control they provide align with the core principles of decentralization that underpin the world of digital assets. While paper wallets offer exceptional security against online threats, they require careful handling and physical safeguarding to prevent damage or loss. Adhering to best practices and key considerations can maximize the security of funds stored in paper wallets and ensure that this traditional yet effective method continues to preserve wealth in the fast-paced and transformative world of cryptocurrencies. As technology evolves, paper wallets remain a steadfast and reliable option for safeguarding digital fortunes and embodying the essence of true ownership and control in the cryptocurrency ecosystem.

Best practices for securing your cryptocurrencies

As cryptocurrencies continue to disrupt traditional finance and gain widespread adoption, securing digital assets has become a paramount concern for cryptocurrency holders. With the decentralization and pseudonymity of cryptocurrencies, the responsibility for safeguarding funds falls directly on the users themselves.

The first and most crucial step in securing cryptocurrencies is choosing the right wallet. Hardware and software wallets have their merits, but regardless of the type, it is essential to use reputable and well-established wallets with a history of robust security measures. Hardware wallets like Ledger and Trezor provide an offline and isolated environment for storing private keys, offering enhanced protection against online threats. On the other hand, software wallets like Electrum and MyEtherWallet can also be secure if users follow strict security practices. Whichever wallet type is chosen, regularly updating the wallet software and firmware ensures that the latest security patches are in place.

Password security is an often underestimated aspect of cryptocurrency protection. Using strong, unique, and complex passwords is vital for preventing unauthorized access to wallets and accounts. Password managers can be valuable tools to generate and store strong passwords securely. It is crucial to avoid using common passwords or easily guessable information, including birthdates or names, and refrain from reusing passwords across different platforms. Additionally, enabling multi-factor authentication (MFA) wherever possible adds a further layer of security, requiring users to provide additional verification beyond just a password.

Hardware wallets stand out as one of the most secure cryptocurrency storage options. These physical devices store private keys offline, away from internet-connected devices, making them immune to online threats. Their tamper-resistant features and ability to sign transactions securely offer unparalleled protection. Utilizing a hardware wallet for significant cryptocurrency holdings and long-term storage minimizes the risk of online attacks and enhances the security of digital assets.

Privacy is a significant concern in cryptocurrency, as transactions are recorded on public blockchains, often revealing wallet addresses and transaction amounts. Utilizing privacy coins like Monero or Zcash can offer enhanced transaction privacy. Additionally, employing techniques such as CoinJoin, which combines multiple transactions into a single transaction, can obfuscate the connection between sender and receiver. By avoiding the reuse of addresses and employing privacy-enhancing tools, users can mitigate the risk of unwanted exposure and maintain a higher level of anonymity.

Scammers and fraudsters frequently target cryptocurrency users due to the irreversibility of transactions and the anonymity of blockchain transactions. Common scams include phishing attempts, fake ICOs (Initial Coin Offerings), and Ponzi schemes. Users must stay vigilant and exercise caution when interacting with unfamiliar websites, links, or emails. Verifying the authenticity of wallet addresses and double-checking URLs can prevent falling victim to phishing attacks. Additionally, being skeptical of get-rich-quick schemes and conducting thorough research before investing in any new project can help identify potential scams.

Continuous education is key to staying informed about the most current security threats and best practices in the rapidly evolving cryptocurrency space. Engaging with reputable sources, forums, and communities can provide valuable insights into new security measures and potential risks. Proactively understanding the technical aspects of cryptocurrencies, blockchain technology, and wallet security empowers users to make informed decisions and take necessary safety measures to safeguard their digital wealth effectively.

In the event of device failure, loss, or damage, having secure and redundant backups of private keys or seed phrases is essential for wallet recovery. Users should create multiple backup copies and store them in separate, secure locations. Utilizing fireproof and waterproof safes or bank safety deposit boxes can provide additional protection for these crucial backups.

Staying updated with the latest software updates is crucial for maintaining a secure digital environment. This applies not only to wallet software but also to operating systems, antivirus software, and any other programs used for cryptocurrency-related activities. Regular updates help patch vulnerabilities and enhance the overall security of devices and applications.

Cold storage solutions can provide a layer of protection for long-term storage and significant holdings. Cold storage involves keeping private keys entirely offline on devices not connected to the internet. This isolation mitigates the risk of online attacks and provides an additional safeguard against potential breaches.
While securing cryptocurrencies is essential, adopting responsible trading and investment practices is equally important. Diversifying holdings across different cryptocurrencies and assets can mitigate risks associated with market volatility. Employing stop-loss orders and setting realistic investment goals helps manage risk and prevent significant losses.

In conclusion, securing cryptocurrencies demands proactive measures and adherence to best practices. By choosing reputable wallets, employing strong password management, utilizing hardware wallets, enhancing privacy measures, being vigilant against scams, pursuing ongoing education, creating secure backups, and regularly updating software, users can fortify their digital wealth against potential threats. Embracing responsible trading practices and risk management further complements the overall security of cryptocurrency holdings. In the ever-evolving landscape of cryptocurrencies, a proactive and educated approach to security empowers users to confidently navigate the world of digital finance and protect their valuable assets from potential risks.

CHAPTER VI

Cryptocurrency Mining

What is cryptocurrency mining?

In the realm of cryptocurrencies, mining is a fundamental concept underpinning blockchain technology's very fabric. Often dubbed the "digital gold rush," cryptocurrency mining involves validating and securing transactions on decentralized networks through complex mathematical computations.

At its core, cryptocurrency mining serves two primary purposes: achieving consensus and maintaining the security of the underlying blockchain network. Mining acts as a decentralized consensus mechanism in decentralized cryptocurrencies like Bitcoin, where there is no central authority to verify transactions. Miners compete to solve intricate mathematical puzzles to validate transactions, agree on the order of transactions in a block, and add new blocks to the blockchain. By reaching a consensus on the state of the network, miners prevent double-spending and ensure the integrity of the distributed ledger.

The mining process involves solving cryptographic puzzles through a process known as Proof of Work (PoW). In PoW-based cryptocurrencies like Bitcoin and Litecoin, miners use powerful computational hardware to solve the puzzles, searching for a specific nonce (a number) that, when hashed with the data in a block, generates a hash value below a target difficulty level. The next block is added to the blockchain by the first miner to discover the correct solution, and they are rewarded with newly created cryptocurrency and transaction fees.

Mining hardware plays a crucial role in determining a miner's success. Initially, mining was possible using ordinary CPUs, but the introduction of Graphics Processing Units, or GPUs and Application-Specific Integrated Circuits (ASICs) revolutionized the industry. GPUs and ASICs are significantly more efficient at solving mining puzzles, making mining with CPUs impractical. Mining software provides the necessary interface to connect mining hardware to the cryptocurrency network. Popular mining software includes CGMiner, BFGMiner, and Easyminer.

One of the most debated aspects of cryptocurrency mining is its energy consumption. Mining requires substantial computing power, which, in turn, demands a considerable amount of electricity. As a result, mining operations consume significant energy resources, raising concerns about their environmental impact. Countries with abundant and cheap electricity often become hotspots for mining activity. However, some cryptocurrencies are exploring alternatives to PoW, such as Proof of Authority (PoA) or Proof of Stake (PoS), which consume significantly less energy.

With the increasing difficulty of mining puzzles and the rising hardware cost, solo mining has become less feasible for individual miners. As a response, mining pools have emerged, allowing miners to combine their computing power and work collectively to solve puzzles. When a pool successfully mines a block, the rewards are distributed among participants based on their contributions. Popular mining pools include Antpool, F2Pool, and Slush Pool.

The landscape of cryptocurrency mining is continually evolving. As mining technology advances, there is a constant race to develop more efficient and powerful mining hardware. Additionally, the growing concerns over energy consumption have led to innovations in mining operations that rely on renewable energy sources to mitigate the environmental impact. Furthermore, the shift towards alternative consensus mechanisms, like PoS, seeks to address energy consumption concerns and reduce the reliance on energy-intensive mining processes.

In conclusion, cryptocurrency mining is the backbone of decentralized cryptocurrencies, ensuring consensus and security within the network. Through complex mathematical computations, miners validate transactions, secure the blockchain, and mint new coins. Mining hardware and software continue to evolve, optimizing efficiency and enhancing mining capabilities. However, concerns over energy consumption have prompted the exploration of alternative consensus mechanisms. As the cryptocurrency ecosystem evolves, mining will undoubtedly remain critical, driving innovation and powering the digital revolution.

Proof of Work vs. Proof of Stake

In cryptocurrencies, consensus mechanisms play a vital role in determining how transactions are validated and new blocks are added to the blockchain. Two prominent consensus mechanisms, Proof of Work (PoW) and Proof of Stake (PoS), have emerged as the cornerstones of blockchain technology.

Proof of Work was introduced with the creation of Bitcoin by the anonymous pseudonymous Satoshi Nakamoto in

2009. PoW relies on miners competing to solve complex mathematical puzzles to verify transactions and add new blocks to the blockchain. The first miner to complete the puzzle gets the opportunity to add the block and gets a reward in the form of freshly minted coins and transaction fees. PoW's security lies in the computational effort required to solve these puzzles, making it costly and time- consuming for attackers to gain control over the network. Bitcoin's PoW mechanism has been remarkably successful in maintaining a secure and decentralized network, but it comes with significant energy consumption concerns due to the intensive computational calculations involved.

Proof of Stake or PoS, is an alternative consensus mechanism that addresses some of the concerns associated with PoW, particularly its energy consumption. Instead of relying on computational work, PoS operates on the principle of validators staking their cryptocurrency holdings as collateral to participate in the block validation process. The probability of a validator being chosen to create the next block is directly proportional to the number of coins they have staked. By staking their coins as collateral, validators are incentivized to act honestly and in the network's best interest, as malicious behavior could result in the loss of their staked coins.

Proof of Work has several advantages that contribute to its robustness and security. Firstly, PoW has proven itself over time, as demonstrated by the resilience and security of the Bitcoin network since its inception. The consensus mechanism is inherently decentralized, allowing anyone with the necessary computational power to participate in mining and validating transactions. Additionally, PoW incentivizes miners to follow the rules, as attempting to manipulate the blockchain would require an enormous amount of computational resources and would likely be economically unfeasible. However, PoW's energy consumption has become a significant concern, as the energy-intensive mining process has raised questions about its environmental impact and sustainability.

Proof of Stake offers several advantages over PoW, with energy efficiency being one of the most notable. Unlike PoW, which requires constant computational power, PoS does not demand significant energy consumption, making it a more environmentally friendly consensus mechanism. The reduced energy consumption also leads to cost savings, as validators do not need to invest in expensive mining hardware. PoS also contributes to decentralization, allowing a wider pool of participants with different amounts of staked coins to take part in the block validation process.

However, PoS is not without its challenges. One of the main concerns with PoS is the "rich get richer" problem, where those with more significant stakes have a higher probability of being chosen to validate blocks and receive rewards. This can lead to centralization, as a few wealthy individuals or entities may control a significant portion of the network. To address this issue, some PoS cryptocurrencies implement coin age or randomization measures to ensure a fair and more decentralized distribution of block validation opportunities.

The debate between PoW and PoS centers around the trade-off between decentralization and security. PoW has demonstrated its ability to maintain a highly decentralized and secure network, as evidenced by the success of Bitcoin. However, PoW's energy consumption raises concerns about sustainability and environmental impact. PoS, on the other hand, offers a more energy-efficient alternative, but critics argue that it may compromise decentralization if a small number of entities hold a significant portion of the stake.

The PoW-PoS debate is ongoing, and various blockchain projects are exploring hybrid consensus mechanisms that combine elements of both PoW and PoS to achieve a balance between security, decentralization, and energy efficiency.

Scalability is another significant challenge for both PoW and PoS. As cryptocurrencies gain popularity and transaction volumes increase, the ability of the network to handle a high number of transactions becomes crucial. PoW's energy-intensive nature can limit its scalability, as it becomes increasingly difficult and costly to process many transactions. PoS, while more energy-efficient, also faces scalability challenges if the network becomes congested with many validators attempting to create new blocks simultaneously.

The future of blockchain consensus will likely be diverse, with different cryptocurrencies adopting various consensus mechanisms based on their specific needs and goals. PoW will likely remain a dominant consensus mechanism for cryptocurrencies like Bitcoin, prioritizing security and decentralization. However, PoS and other alternative consensus mechanisms will likely continue to gain traction, especially for projects that value energy efficiency, scalability, and environmental sustainability. In

conclusion, the debate between Proof of Work and Proof of Stake represents a critical turning point in the evolution of blockchain technology. While PoW has proven itself as a secure and decentralized consensus mechanism, its energy consumption has become a cause for concern. PoS offers an energy-efficient alternative but faces challenges related to decentralization and scalability. The future of blockchain consensus will likely be shaped by hybrid approaches that strive to balance security, decentralization, energy efficiency, and scalability. As the cryptocurrency ecosystem continues to evolve, consensus mechanisms will play a crucial role in shaping the future of digital finance and revolutionizing various industries worldwide.

Mining process and requirements

Cryptocurrency mining is at the core of blockchain technology, serving as the backbone for validating transactions and securing the decentralized network. This section delves into the intricacies of the mining process, exploring the requirements, hardware and software components, mining algorithms, and the challenges miners face. By unraveling the mechanics of cryptocurrency mining, we gain insight into its vital role in the world of digital finance.

The mining process begins when transactions are propagated across the network. Miners collect these transactions and package them into blocks, which are essentially a batch of transactions waiting to be added to the blockchain. Each block has a reference to the previous block's hash, creating a chain of blocks - the blockchain.

Mining hardware plays a pivotal role in the mining process. In the early days of cryptocurrencies, mining could be performed using standard CPUs, but as the complexity of mining puzzles increased, miners quickly turned to more powerful graphics cards, known as Graphics Processing Units (GPUs). GPUs provided significant computational power and sped up the mining process. However, with the rise of ASICs (Application-Specific Integrated Circuits), the mining landscape changed drastically. ASICs are specialized mining machines designed to perform the specific calculations required for mining a particular cryptocurrency. These devices significantly outperform GPUs in terms of efficiency and speed, leading to increased competition among miners.

Mining hardware alone is insufficient for successful mining; miners also require mining software to connect their hardware to the blockchain network. Mining software acts as an interface, facilitating communication between the miner's hardware and the network. Popular mining software includes CGMiner, BFGMiner, and Easyminer, each with its unique features and optimizations. Mining software helps miners monitor their mining operations, track performance, and receive real-time updates on the blockchain network.

Each cryptocurrency has a mining algorithm, determining the specific computational puzzles miners must solve. For instance, Bitcoin uses the SHA-256 algorithm, Litecoin uses Scrypt, and Ethereum uses Ethash. These algorithms are designed to be computationally intensive, ensuring that mining requires substantial computing power and thus, discourages malicious actors from attempting to gain control of the network.

Mining cryptocurrencies demand significant computational power, and this comes at a cost - electricity consumption. The energy-intensive nature of mining has raised concerns about its environmental impact, particularly for cryptocurrencies that rely on PoW. Miners need to strike a delicate balance between the profitability of their mining operations and the cost of electricity. Mining operations often seek locations with access to cheap and abundant electricity, which has led to the concentration of mining activities in certain regions, such as China, where coal power is plentiful.

As mining became more competitive and the complexity of mining puzzles increased, solo mining became less viable for individual miners. As a result, mining pools were created as a way for miners to join together and pool their computational power in order to improve their probability of finding a block. Rewards are given to members of a mining pool according to how much they have contributed to the pool's total hash rate after the pool successfully mines a block. Popular mining pools include Antpool, F2Pool, and Slush Pool.

Mining is not without its challenges. The increasing difficulty of mining puzzles demands ever more powerful and efficient hardware, leading to higher costs for miners. The constant advancements in mining technology mean miners must stay updated with the latest hardware to remain competitive. Additionally, the reward halving events in some cryptocurrencies, like Bitcoin, reduce the block reward over time, impacting the profitability of mining operations.

In conclusion, the mining process is the backbone of blockchain technology, responsible for validating transactions and securing the decentralized network. It involves solving complex cryptographic puzzles through Proof of Work algorithms, requiring substantial computational power. Miners invest in specialized mining hardware, such as ASICs, to enhance their mining efficiency. Mining software serves as an interface to the blockchain network, allowing miners to monitor their operations and receive real-time updates. Mining consumes an extensive amount of electricity, leading to concerns about its environmental impact. To mitigate challenges and increase their chances of success, miners join mining pools, combining their computational power. Despite the hurdles, mining remains an essential and integral aspect of cryptocurrencies, shaping the future of digital finance and revolutionizing various industries worldwide.

Environmental impact of mining

Cryptocurrency mining, a fundamental process in blockchain technology, has revolutionized the financial landscape. However, it comes with a significant environmental cost. This section delves into the environmental impact of mining, exploring the factors contributing to its ecological footprint, challenges, and potential solutions for a sustainable future. By understanding the environmental implications, we can work towards mitigating the negative effects and promoting eco-friendly mining practices.

One of the primary contributors to the environmental impact of mining is its energy consumption. Mining cryptocurrencies like Bitcoin and Ethereum involves solving complex cryptographic puzzles through the energy-intensive Proof of Work (PoW) algorithm. The mining hardware, often specialized ASICs, requires vast amounts of electricity to perform the numerous calculations needed for mining. As mining difficulty increases, miners continuously upgrade their hardware, further driving up energy consumption.

The energy requirements for mining have led to the concentration of mining activities in regions with access to cheap electricity, often sourced from non-renewable energy sources like coal or natural gas. This reliance on fossil fuels exacerbates carbon emissions and contributes to global warming, making mining a major contributor to the carbon footprint of the cryptocurrency industry.

The rapid evolution of mining hardware results in older models becoming obsolete, leading to a growing problem of electronic waste (e-waste). As miners upgrade their equipment to stay competitive, older hardware is often discarded, adding to the mounting e-waste problem. Many electronic devices has hazardous components that can impair the environment and human health if not properly disposed.

E-waste recycling and responsible disposal are essential to mitigate the environmental impact of mining. Implementing recycling programs, incentivizing responsible hardware disposal, and promoting circular economy practices can help address this growing concern.

In regions with abundant cheap electricity, mining operations often rely on non-renewable energy sources like coal or natural gas. To meet the increasing energy demands of mining, power plants may expand, leading to deforestation and changes in land use. The clearing of forests for mining-related infrastructure can lead to the biodiversity loss, disruption of ecosystems, and exacerbate climate change.

Promoting the utilization of renewable energy sources, like solar, wind, or hydroelectric power, can significantly reduce the environmental impact of mining. By transitioning towards sustainable energy alternatives, miners can mitigate their contribution to deforestation and land degradation.

Mining hardware generates substantial heat, necessitating extensive cooling systems to maintain optimal performance. These cooling systems often rely on water, contributing to significant water usage by mining operations. In regions with scarce water resources, such high consumption can strain local water supplies and harm aquatic ecosystems.

Efficient cooling technologies and water recycling practices can help reduce water consumption in mining operations. Implementing water management strategies prioritizing conservation and sustainability can mitigate the environmental impact on local water resources.

Mining facilities often release air pollutants, such as greenhouse gases and particulate matter, during the process of generating electricity for mining operations. Burning fossil fuels in power plants releases carbon dioxide (CO_2), methane (CH_4), and other greenhouse gases, contributing to air pollution and climate change. Transitioning to renewable energy sources reduces greenhouse gas emissions and improves air quality, benefiting the environment and the health of nearby communities.

Addressing the environmental impact of mining requires collective efforts from the cryptocurrency industry, governments, and environmental organizations. Several strategies can promote eco-friendly mining practices and foster sustainability within the industry.

Adopting renewable energy sources is crucial to reducing the carbon footprint of mining. Governments and mining companies can collaborate to incentivize the utilization of renewable energy through subsidies, tax breaks, or green energy certificates. Integrating renewable energy into mining operations benefits the environment and ensures the long-term viability of mining as an industry.

Regulatory frameworks that promote sustainable mining practices can be pivotal in mitigating the environmental impact of mining. Governments can impose energy efficiency standards, mandate responsible e-waste disposal, and encourage water conservation in mining operations. Striking the right balance between fostering technological innovation and protecting the environment is essential for the long-term sustainability of the cryptocurrency industry.

Mining companies can engage with local communities and environmental organizations to understand the potential impact of mining on the surrounding ecosystem. Responsible land use and environmental management plans can help minimize disruptions to habitats and biodiversity.

Investing in research and innovation can lead to developing greener mining technologies and more energy-efficient hardware. The cryptocurrency community can support projects exploring alternative consensus mechanisms, like Proof of Stake, which consumes significantly less energy than PoW.

In conclusion, the environmental impact of mining in cryptocurrency is a significant concern that demands urgent attention. The energy-intensive nature of mining, coupled with e-waste disposal and land use challenges, requires proactive measures to promote eco-friendly mining practices.

By embracing renewable energy, implementing sustainable mining policies, and engaging with local communities, the cryptocurrency industry can pave the way for a more sustainable and greener future. As the industry continues to grow and evolve, prioritizing environmental responsibility can help preserve our planet

while harnessing the potential of blockchain technology
for positive change.

CHAPTER VII

Analyzing Cryptocurrencies

Fundamental analysis

Cryptocurrencies have captivated the financial world, presenting opportunities and challenges for investors. Amidst the volatile market, fundamental analysis emerges as a key tool to decipher cryptocurrencies' underlying value and potential. This section explores the principles of fundamental analysis, its core metrics, and its significance in making informed investment decisions in the ever-evolving cryptocurrency landscape.

Fundamental analysis is a method that is used to evaluate the intrinsic value of an asset, including cryptocurrencies. Unlike technical analysis, which relies on price charts and historical data, fundamental analysis examines the underlying factors that drive a cryptocurrency value. By studying the project's technology, team, use case, and market demand, fundamental analysis aims to gauge the asset's long-term potential.

The technology behind a cryptocurrency is a fundamental aspect of its value. Assessing a project's blockchain infrastructure, consensus mechanism, and scalability provides valuable insights into its sustainability and potential for mass adoption. For example, a cryptocurrency with a robust and efficient blockchain is more likely to handle high transaction volumes and gain traction in real-world applications.

The development team are crucial in the success of a cryptocurrency project. Evaluating the expertise, experience, and credibility of the team members provides an understanding of their ability to deliver on promises and navigate technological challenges. A team with a strong track record and a clear roadmap inspires confidence in the project's long-term viability.

The practicality and relevance of a cryptocurrency's use case are vital in determining its potential value. Projects that address real-world problems and offer innovative solutions are more likely to gain widespread adoption and investor interest. Understanding a cryptocurrency's target market and potential applications provides valuable insights into its growth prospects.

The cryptocurrency community's interest and support are crucial factors in the success of a project. Monitoring social media trends, community engagement, and developer activity can help gauge a cryptocurrency's level of interest and adoption. A strong and active community often indicates a vibrant and promising project.

A cryptocurrency's economic model and tokenomics determine its supply and demand dynamics. A deflationary model, where the token supply decreases over time, can create scarcity and drive up demand, potentially leading to price appreciation. Conversely, an inflationary model may result in a steady decrease in value over time. Understanding the token distribution, inflation rate, and overall economic model is essential in evaluating a cryptocurrency's long-term potential.

The regulatory environment significantly impacts the cryptocurrency market. Governments' policies and regulations can influence the adoption and growth of cryptocurrencies in different jurisdictions. Projects that comply with regulatory requirements and have a clear legal framework are better positioned to weather regulatory challenges and gain legitimacy.

There is intense competition among the many projects in the cryptocurrency sector for investors' attention and investment. Conducting a competitive analysis helps identify a project's unique selling points and differentiators. Understanding how a cryptocurrency stacks up against its competitors provides valuable insights into its potential market share and competitive advantage.

Evaluating a cryptocurrency project's financial health is crucial in assessing its viability and long-term sustainability. Examining factors such as funding sources, revenue models, and financial transparency helps investors understand how a project manages its resources and sustains its operations.

While fundamental analysis focuses on objective data, sentiment analysis delves into the subjective aspect of investor sentiment and market psychology. Understanding market sentiment can provide insights into short-term price movements and potential market trends. Sentiment analysis often complements fundamental analysis to gain a comprehensive market view.

In conclusion, fundamental analysis plays a pivotal role in evaluating the value and potential of cryptocurrencies. By examining the technology, development team, use case, market demand, economic model, regulatory landscape, and competitive positioning, investors can make informed decisions in the ever-evolving cryptocurrency landscape. As the cryptocurrency market matures, fundamental analysis remains essential for identifying promising projects and distinguishing them from speculative ventures. Combining fundamental analysis with risk management strategies empowers investors to navigate the volatile market, seize opportunities, and build robust portfolios that align with their long-term investment goals.

However, it is essential to acknowledge that fundamental analysis is not foolproof, and the cryptocurrency market is inherently speculative and subject to rapid changes. Therefore, investors should cautiously approach cryptocurrency investment, diversify their holdings, and stay informed about market developments. In doing so, investors can harness the power of fundamental analysis to navigate the exciting and transformative world of cryptocurrencies while mitigating risks and maximizing potential rewards.

Technical analysis

Cryptocurrencies have taken the financial world by storm, captivating investors with their potential for high returns and market volatility. Amidst this rapidly changing landscape, technical analysis has emerged as a powerful tool for analyzing cryptocurrencies. This section explores the principles of technical analysis, its core concepts, and its significance in deciphering market trends and price patterns to make informed investment decisions in the dynamic world of digital assets.

Technical analysis is a method that is used in evaluating financial assets, including cryptocurrencies, by studying historical price data and market trends. It is founded on the premise that market trends and price patterns repeat over time. By analyzing price action, trading volume, and other market indicators, technical analysis seeks to predict future price movements and identify potential purchasing or selling opportunities.

Price charts, particularly candlestick charts, are the primary tools used in technical analysis. Candlestick charts display the price movements of cryptocurrencies over specific timeframes, providing a visual representation of market trends. By studying candlestick patterns, analysts can identify bullish (upward) and bearish (downward) trends and potential trend reversals.

Support and resistance levels are vital concepts in technical analysis. Support levels are price levels at which a cryptocurrency's price has historically found buying interest, preventing it from falling further. On the other hand, resistance levels are price levels at which selling pressure has historically emerged, preventing the price from rising. Identifying support and resistance levels helps traders decide on entry and exit points.

Moving averages are widely used technical indicators that help smooth out price data to identify trends more effectively. Simple Moving Averages (or SMA) and Exponential Moving Averages (or EMA) are the two common types used in technical analysis. Moving averages can signal potential trend changes and provide insights into the cryptocurrency's overall price direction.

The momentum oscillator known as the Relative Strength Index, or RSI, measures the rate of change and rapidity of market movements. The range of RSI values is 0 to 100; values over 70 suggest overbought situations, while values below 30 suggest oversold conditions. The RSI helps traders identify potential market reversals and evaluate the strength of a cryptocurrency's price momentum.

One momentum indicator that follows trends and aids traders in identifying shifts in trends is the Moving Average Convergence Divergence, or MACD. The signal line and the MACD line make up its two lines. A potential bullish trend is indicated when the MACD line crosses over the signal line; a potential bearishtrend is indicated when the MACD line crosses below the signal line.

Technical indicators called Bollinger Bands are used to gauge market volatility and spot possible breakouts. They are made up of three lines: the middle band, which is typically just a simple moving average, the upper, and lower band. When the price moves close to the upper band, it may indicate an overbought condition, while a move close to the lower band may suggest an oversold condition.

Based on the Fibonacci sequence, Fibonacci retracement levels are a useful tool for determining possible levels of support and resistance. These levels are used by traders to identify areas of interest in buying or selling, as well as probable price reversal points. Fibonacci retracement levels are prevalent in technical analysis and often coincide with significant price movements.

The Ichimoku Cloud, also known as Ichimoku Kinko Hyo, is a comprehensive technical indicator that provides a holistic view of a cryptocurrency's price action. It consists of five lines: Tenkan-sen, Kijun-sen, Senkou Span A, Senkou Span B, and Chikou Span. One can utilize the Ichimoku Cloud to find trends, levels of support and resistance, and possible entry and exit points.

Technical analysis has limitations even though it's a useful technique for studying cryptocurrencies. The subjectivity of interpretation and the potential for false signals are inherent challenges in technical analysis. Additionally, the cryptocurrency market's inherent volatility and susceptibility to external factors can make it unpredictable, even for experienced analysts.

To overcome the limitations of each analysis method, many traders and investors adopt a comprehensive approach by combining technical and fundamental analysis. By using both methods, they gain a more complete understanding of a cryptocurrency's potential, considering both its underlying value and the market sentiment.

In conclusion, technical analysis is a potent tool for analyzing cryptocurrencies and navigating the dynamic and volatile market. Traders can acquire insights into market trends and price patterns by studying price charts, candlestick patterns, support and resistance levels, moving averages, and various technical indicators. While technical analysis is valuable in making informed investment decisions, it should be used with other analytical methods, such as fundamental analysis and risk management strategies. No analysis method can predict market movements with absolute certainty, but by leveraging technical analysis alongside a comprehensive approach, traders can enhance their understanding and decision-making in the thrilling world of cryptocurrencies.

Evaluating market trends and patterns

Cryptocurrencies, a revolutionary asset class, have captured the attention of investors worldwide with their potential for massive returns and unprecedented market volatility. Amidst this dynamic landscape, understanding market trends and patterns is crucial to analyzing cryptocurrencies. Market trends lay the foundation of technical analysis in cryptocurrency trading. A trend is the general direction in which an asset's price is moving over time. There are three main trends in cryptocurrency markets: uptrend, downtrend, and sideways (also known as range-bound). Identifying and understanding the prevailing trend is essential, providing critical insights for traders and investors.

Technical indicators are mathematical computations derived from historical volume and price data. These indicators are invaluable tools for evaluating market trends and patterns. Popular technical indicators used in cryptocurrency analysis include Moving Averages (MA), Relative Strength Index (RSI), Moving Average Convergence Divergence (MACD), Bollinger Bands, and Fibonacci Retracement. Each indicator offers unique insights into market dynamics and helps traders identify potential entry and exit points.

Support and resistance levels are vital concepts in analyzing market trends and patterns. Support refers to a price level where a cryptocurrency's price historically tends to find buying interest, preventing it from falling further. On the other hand, resistance is a price level where selling pressure has historically emerged, preventing the price from rising. These levels are vital in assessing potential price reversals and charting future price movements.

Price movements that repeat over time are shown visually in chart patterns. These patterns offer valuable insights into market sentiment and potential price trends. Some common chart patterns are Head and Shoulders, Double Tops and Bottoms, Triangles, Flags, and Pennants. By recognizing these patterns, traders can anticipate possible price movements and adjust their strategies accordingly.

Moving Averages (MA) are technical indicators that efficiently smooth out price data to identify trends. Simple Moving Averages (SMA) and Exponential Moving Averages (EMA) are the two main types of moving averages used in cryptocurrency analysis. Traders frequently use moving averages to identify trends' strength and direction and spot potential trend reversals.

The Relative Strength Index (or RSI) and Moving Average Convergence Divergence (or MACD) are momentum indicators that help traders assess the strength and sustainability of a trend. RSI gauges the speed and change of price movements, while MACD detects trend changes and momentum shifts. By using these indicators, traders can gauge the market's momentum and make informed trading decisions.

Fibonacci Retracement is a technical tool based on the Fibonacci sequence. It helps traders identify probable support and resistance levels based on specific percentage retracements of a cryptocurrency's price movement. By plotting these retracement levels on a price chart, traders can anticipate potential price reversal points and determine strategic entry and exit levels.

Price movements throughout particular timeframes are visually represented by candlestick patterns. These patterns display an asset's opening, closing, high, and low prices and are widely used in technical analysis. Candlestick patterns, such as Doji, Hammer, and Engulfing, offer beneficial insights into market sentiment and potential trend reversals.

Volume is an essential indicator used in conjunction with price analysis. Volume represents the number of cryptocurrency units traded during a specific period. An increase in trading volume often confirms the strength of a trend, while declining volume may indicate a potential trend reversal.

Sentiment analysis involves gauging market participants' emotions and attitudes towards cryptocurrencies. It complements technical analysis by providing insights into investor sentiment, which can influence price movements. Social media platforms, forums, and news sentiment analysis are commonly used to assess market psychology.

Advancements in technology have brought machine learning and artificial intelligence (AI) to the forefront of cryptocurrency market analysis. These technologies can analyze vast amounts of historical data, identify patterns, and make forecasts based on complex algorithms. Machine learning models are used to forecast price movements and assist traders in making more data-driven decisions.

In conclusion, evaluating market trends and patterns is fundamental to analyzing cryptocurrencies. Traders and investors can acquire valuable insights into price movements and market behavior by understanding market trends, using technical indicators, recognizing chart patterns, and considering sentiment analysis. Technical analysis provides a structured approach to understanding market dynamics and making informed trading decisions. However, it is crucial to acknowledge that no analysis method is foolproof, and the cryptocurrency market is inherently volatile and unpredictable. Combining technical analysis with risk management strategies, fundamental analysis, and market research is essential for a comprehensive understanding of the ever-changing cryptocurrency landscape. By harnessing the power of market trends and patterns, market participants can navigate the exciting world of cryptocurrencies more confidently and maximize their potential for success in this dynamic and rapidly developing market.

CHAPTER VIII

Understanding Market Volatility

Factors influencing cryptocurrency price fluctuations

Blockchain technology has completely changed the banking industry by providing a digital, decentralized substitute for fiat money. The tremendous price volatility of cryptocurrencies is one of their distinguishing features. Prices can drop dramatically or soar to unimaginable heights in a matter of hours. In order to make wise judgments in this dynamic and rapidly evolving market, traders and investors must have a thorough understanding of the variables impacting cryptocurrency price fluctuations.

Market demand and supply dynamics play a significant role in shaping cryptocurrency prices. When there is high demand for a particular cryptocurrency and a limited supply, its price tends to increase. Conversely, when demand wanes or supply increases, the price may decrease. Market sentiment, news, and events can trigger shifts in demand and supply, leading to sudden price fluctuations.

The underlying technology and development progress of a cryptocurrency significantly impact its price. Technological advancements, upgrades, and improvements enhance the utility and scalability of a cryptocurrency, making it more attractive to investors and users. Positive developments often result in price appreciation, while technological setbacks or vulnerabilities can lead to price declines.

The regulatory landscape plays a pivotal role in shaping cryptocurrency prices. Government policies, legal frameworks, and regulatory announcements can lead to positive and negative price movements. Positive regulatory developments, such as recognizing cryptocurrencies as legal tender, can boost investor confidence and drive prices upward. Conversely, strict regulations or outright bans in certain jurisdictions may result in price declines.

Media coverage and news events have a profound influence on cryptocurrency prices. Positive news, such as adoption by major companies or government endorsements, can trigger price surges. Conversely, negative news, like security breaches or regulatory breakdowns, can cause significant price drops. Traders and investors closely monitor news sources and media platforms to stay ahead of potential price movements.

The cryptocurrency market is quite speculative and subject to the sentiment and psychology of investors. Fear, uncertainty, and greed are powerful emotions that can lead to herd behavior and price bubbles. Positive market sentiment may lead to FOMO (Fear Of Missing Out), driving prices to unsustainable levels, while negative sentiment can trigger panic selling and steep price declines.

Market liquidity, the simplicity with which an asset can be purchased or sold, and trading volumes are critical in cryptocurrency price fluctuations. Low liquidity and trading volumes can lead to price manipulation and sharp price swings. Large buy or sell orders can cause significant price movements in illiquid markets.

Cryptocurrencies are not isolated from global economic trends and events. Economic crises, geopolitical tensions, inflation, and currency devaluation in traditional financial markets can influence investors' perception of cryptocurrencies as alternative assets or safe-haven investments. In times of economic uncertainty, cryptocurrencies may experience increased interest and price appreciation.

The strength and reputation of a cryptocurrency's development team and community support can impact its price. A robust, transparent, and dedicated development team inspires confidence in the project's future prospects. Active community support indicates a vibrant and engaged user base, which can attract more investors and positively impact the price.

Cryptocurrency markets are susceptible to manipulation by large holders, often referred to as "whales." Whales have substantial holdings of a particular cryptocurrency and can influence prices by strategically buying or selling large amounts. Market manipulation practices like pump-and-dump schemes can create artificial price movements and pose risks for unsuspecting traders.

Technological or security concerns can influence cryptocurrency prices. Security breaches, hacks, or vulnerabilities in the underlying technology can erode investor confidence and lead to price declines. On the other hand, advancements in security measures can enhance trust and positively impact prices.

As cryptocurrencies gain mainstream recognition, their interconnectivity with traditional financial markets grows. Events in the stock, forex, or commodity markets can spill over into the cryptocurrency market and influence prices. Investors often diversify their portfolios by incorporating cryptocurrencies, leading to correlations between various markets.

The scarcity of specific cryptocurrencies, such as Bitcoin's capped supply at 21 million coins, can influence prices positively. As demand for a limited supply increases, prices tend to rise. Additionally, halving events in cryptocurrencies like Bitcoin, which reduce the block rewards for miners, can impact supply dynamics and potentially lead to price appreciation.

In conclusion, understanding the factors influencing cryptocurrency price fluctuations is a complex and ever-evolving endeavor. The cryptocurrency market is quite speculative and subject to internal and external influences. Factors like market demand and supply dynamics, technological advancements, regulatory environment, media coverage, market sentiment, liquidity, global economic conditions, development team and community support, market manipulation, security concerns, and interconnectivity with traditional financial markets all play a crucial role in shaping cryptocurrency prices.

Investors and traders must cautiously approach the cryptocurrency market and conduct thorough research. Analyzing a combination of fundamental factors and technical indicators can help make more informed investment decisions. While cryptocurrency investing offers exciting opportunities, it is essential to acknowledge the inherent risks and volatility. By staying informed and adopting a disciplined approach, market participants can navigate this ever-changing landscape with greater confidence and prudence.

Strategies for managing market volatility

Cryptocurrencies have gained immense popularity recently, attracting many investors seeking lucrative opportunities. However, this burgeoning market comes with its share of challenges, most notably its extreme price volatility. Cryptocurrency prices can experience rapid and unpredictable fluctuations, leaving investors vulnerable to significant gains or losses. Understanding and implementing strategies for managing market volatility is crucial to navigating the turbulent waters of the cryptocurrency market.

A basic risk management technique called diversification distributes investments among a number of different assets or cryptocurrencies. By diversifying their portfolios, investors can mitigate the impact of price fluctuations in any single cryptocurrency. Different cryptocurrencies may have unique market dynamics, and their prices may not move in sync. Consequently, a well-diversified portfolio can help cushion the impact of losses in one cryptocurrency with gains in another.

Before venturing into the cryptocurrency market, investors must assess their risk tolerance. The volatility of cryptocurrencies can be emotionally taxing, leading to impulsive decision-making and potential losses. Understanding one's risk appetite and capacity can help in designing a suitable investment strategy. Some individuals may prefer a conservative approach, focusing on more established and less volatile cryptocurrencies, while others might be willing to take higher risks for potential higher rewards.

Regardless of the price of a cryptocurrency, dollar-cost averaging (DCA) is a systematic investment approach that involves buying a set quantity of the asset at regular intervals. This approach helps investors avoid the pitfalls of trying to time the market. By consistently buying cryptocurrencies over time, investors can obtain an average cost that smooths out the impact of short-term price volatility.

In volatile markets, stop-loss orders are a vital tool for risk management. When a cryptocurrency's price hits a predefined level, these orders automatically cause it to be sold. By setting a stop-loss order, investors can limit their potential losses in case the price of a cryptocurrency experiences a sudden decline. Stop-loss orders can be beneficial during periods of heightened market volatility.

Take-profit orders work in the opposite way of stop-loss orders. They allow investors to set a target price at which they wish to sell their cryptocurrencies to secure profits. Take-profit orders are useful in volatile markets where prices can surge and then quickly reverse. Investors can lock in gains by setting a take-profit order before prices potentially retreat.

Market volatility can be unnerving for short-term traders who attempt to profit from short-lived price swings. Adopting a long-term investment perspective can help investors weather the storm of market volatility. Instead of reacting to short-term price movements, long-term investors focus on the potential of cryptocurrencies over an extended period, considering technological advancements, adoption rates, and utility.

Fundamental analysis involves evaluating the underlying factors that influence a cryptocurrency's value. Factors such as the technology, adoption, use cases, and the team behind a cryptocurrency can provide insights into its potential for long-term growth. By focusing on the fundamentals, investors can make more knowledgeable decisions and resist the urge to react to short-term price fluctuations.

A common method for examining previous price changes and spotting patterns that may indicate to potential future price trends is technical analysis. Traders can make more informed entry and exit decisions by studying historical price data and using technical indicators. Technical analysis can be particularly valuable in predicting short-term price movements, but it also has limitations in the inherently unpredictable cryptocurrency market.

Emotions can be the downfall of many investors in a volatile market. Irrational behavior and hasty decisions might result from fear and greed. Successful cryptocurrency investors resist the need to buy or sell on the basis of emotions by exercising discipline and patience. Developing and sticking to a sound investment plan, regardless of short-term price movements, is essential for long-term success.

In the cryptocurrency market, knowledge is power. Educating oneself about the various cryptocurrencies, market trends, technological developments, and industry news can provide a significant edge. In-depth research allows investors to make informed decisions based on facts and rational analysis rather than speculation. Dollar-Crypto Cost Averaging (DCCA) extends the traditional DCA strategy. It involves converting a fixed amount of fiat currency into cryptocurrencies at regular intervals. This approach helps investors reduce their exposure to the volatility of fiat currencies, which can also experience significant fluctuations in the global market. Hedging involves taking positions or using financial instruments to offset potential losses in a cryptocurrency investment. Options, futures, and other derivatives can be utilized to hedge against adverse price movements. While hedging strategies can be complex and require expertise, they offer additional layers of protection for sophisticated investors.

In conclusion, managing market volatility in the cryptocurrency world requires a combination of prudence, discipline, and strategic planning. Diversification, risk tolerance assessment, dollar-cost averaging, stop-loss and take-profit orders, long-term investment perspectives, fundamental and technical analysis, avoiding emotional trading, research and education, dollar-crypto cost averaging, hedging strategies, and a deep understanding of market dynamics can collectively empower investors to navigate the challenges posed by volatility.

The cryptocurrency market's dynamic nature can create opportunities for substantial gains but also expose investors to significant risks. Investors can survive and thrive in this exciting and ever-changing landscape by employing the right strategies and staying informed. As the cryptocurrency market evolves, so must the strategies for managing volatility, creating a balance between risk and reward for those eager to participate in this revolutionary financial realm.

CHAPTER IX

Cryptocurrency Regulations and Taxes

Global regulatory landscape

Cryptocurrencies have emerged as disruptive in the global financial landscape, offering decentralized and borderless transactions. As this innovative technology gained traction, governments worldwide grappled with the need to regulate this fast-evolving sector. The regulatory landscape for cryptocurrencies is highly fragmented, with countries adopting diverse approaches and attitudes toward digital assets.

Some nations have embraced cryptocurrencies with open arms, recognizing their potential for financial inclusion, economic growth, and technological advancement. These countries often seek to foster innovation and blockchain development through supportive policies and regulations. Conversely, certain jurisdictions have taken a more cautious approach, raising concerns about consumer protection, money laundering, and potential risks associated with cryptocurrencies.

One of the fundamental challenges in the global regulatory landscape is the lack of uniformity in recognizing cryptocurrencies' legal status. Some countries have officially recognized cryptocurrencies as legal tender, enabling businesses to accept them as payment for goods and services. On the other hand, certain countries have outrightly banned cryptocurrencies, citing concerns about their use in illicit activities or potential threats to their national currencies. The diverse legal status of cryptocurrencies creates uncertainty for businesses and investors operating across international borders.

Cryptocurrencies have faced criticism for their potential use in money laundering and terrorist financing. Many countries have introduced Anti-Money Laundering (AML) and Know Your Customer (KYC) regulations for cryptocurrency exchanges and businesses to address these concerns. These regulations require exchanges to validate the identity of their customers and report strange transactions to regulatory authorities. While AML and KYC measures aim to enhance the legitimacy of the cryptocurrency sector, they also impose compliance burdens on businesses and challenge the privacy principles of blockchain technology.

Taxation of cryptocurrencies has been a complex issue for regulators worldwide. Classifying cryptocurrencies as assets, currencies, or commodities determines their tax treatment. Some countries impose capital gains tax on cryptocurrency transactions, while others have introduced specific laws for taxing cryptocurrencies. Additionally, cryptocurrency holders and businesses may have reporting obligations, further adding to the complexities of taxation in this domain.

Cryptocurrencies' inherent volatility and risks have raised concerns about investor protection and consumer rights. Some countries' regulators have warned about the potential risks of investing in cryptocurrencies and encouraged consumers to exercise caution. Others have implemented measures to safeguard investors, such as requiring cryptocurrency issuers to conduct initial coin offerings (ICOs) under specific regulations and guidelines.

As cryptocurrencies gain popularity, regulators are becoming increasingly concerned about their potential impact on financial stability and systemic risk. The substantial capital influx into the cryptocurrency market and the emergence of cryptocurrencies as a new asset class have sparked questions about the relationship between cryptocurrencies and traditional financial systems. The interconnectedness between cryptocurrencies and traditional financial systems presents challenges for regulators in monitoring and managing potential risks.

The borderless nature of cryptocurrencies poses challenges for regulators in overseeing cross-border transactions. Cryptocurrency transactions can occur seamlessly across national boundaries, making it challenging to enforce local regulations. This phenomenon has given rise to regulatory arbitrage, where businesses and investors seek to exploit the differences in regulatory regimes by operating in jurisdictions with favorable cryptocurrency policies.

Some countries have established regulatory sandboxes and innovation hubs in response to the rapidly evolving cryptocurrency industry. These initiatives provide a controlled environment for businesses to test innovative blockchain projects and cryptocurrency-related services. Regulatory sandboxes allow collaboration between regulators and industry stakeholders, fostering a better understanding of the technology's potential and risks. Cryptocurrencies' decentralized and global nature calls for international cooperation and standardization in regulatory efforts. Collaboration between countries can facilitate information exchange, improve enforcement against cross-border illegal activities, and promote consistency in regulatory approaches. Standardization of regulations could also enhance investor confidence and support the sustainable growth of the cryptocurrency market.

One of the most significant challenges in regulating cryptocurrencies is reconciling their decentralized nature with traditional regulatory frameworks. The absence of a central authority in blockchain networks poses unique challenges for regulators. Imposing centralized controls on decentralized systems could undermine the fundamental principles of cryptocurrencies, such as transparency, immutability, and user autonomy.

Regulating cryptocurrencies requires striking a delicate balance between fostering innovation and mitigating risks. While excessive regulation could stifle innovation and drive businesses away, insufficient regulation may expose consumers and investors to potential fraud and abuse. Policymakers must carefully consider cryptocurrencies' potential benefits and risks to design effective and proportionate regulatory frameworks.

As the cryptocurrency industry continues to evolve, the global regulatory landscape will also undergo significant changes. Regulators must adapt to emerging technologies, market dynamics, and investor needs. Striking the right balance between oversight and flexibility will create an enabling environment that encourages innovation and safeguards market participants.

In conclusion, the global regulatory landscape for cryptocurrencies is diverse and complex. Different countries have taken distinct approaches to regulate this transformative technology, leading to fragmented regulatory environments. Challenges such as legal recognition, AML and KYC compliance, taxation, investor protection, financial stability, cross-border transactions, and decentralization are critical issues that regulators must address to foster a healthy and sustainable cryptocurrency market.

As the cryptocurrency industry continues to mature, international cooperation, standardization, and adaptability will play pivotal roles in shaping the future of cryptocurrency regulation. Balancing promoting innovation and protecting consumers is vital for harnessing the potential of cryptocurrencies while mitigating their associated risks. By working collaboratively and keeping pace with technological advancements, regulators can create a regulatory landscape that fosters responsible innovation and supports the global adoption of cryptocurrencies.

Tax implications of cryptocurrency transactions

The introduction of cryptocurrencies has completely changed the financial landscape and presented new challenges for international tax agencies. Understanding the tax implications becomes increasingly crucial as more individuals and businesses engage in cryptocurrency transactions. In many jurisdictions, cryptocurrencies are treated as property rather than traditional currency for tax purposes. Every cryptocurrency transaction, whether buying, selling, trading, or using cryptocurrencies to purchase goods and services, triggers a tax event. As property, the tax treatment of cryptocurrencies is subject to capital gains and losses, requiring taxpayers to accurately report and calculate their gains or losses.

Capital gains tax is a key aspect of the tax implications of cryptocurrency transactions. When taxpayers sell or exchange cryptocurrencies for a higher value than their purchase price, they realize a capital gain. On the other hand, selling or exchanging cryptocurrencies at a lower value results in a capital loss. The distinction between the buying and selling prices is considered the taxable capital gain or loss, which must be reported in the taxpayer's annual tax return. The length of time a taxpayer holds a cryptocurrency before selling or exchanging it can impact the tax rate applied to their capital gains. In many jurisdictions, cryptocurrencies held for less than a certain period (often one year) are subject to short-term capital gains tax, which is commonly taxed at the individual's ordinary income tax rate. On the other hand, cryptocurrencies held for more extended periods may qualify for long-term capital gains tax rates, which are often more favorable.

Cryptocurrency-to-cryptocurrency transactions, such as trading one cryptocurrency for another, also trigger tax events. In such cases, taxpayers must calculate the fair market value of both the original and acquired cryptocurrency at the time of the transaction. The difference between the two values represents the taxable capital gain or loss. Mining cryptocurrency involves producing new coins and confirming transactions, and it may have tax repercussions. Revenue from mining is often handled like regular income and is liable to income tax at the time of receipt. Miners may also incur mining-related expenses, such as electricity and equipment costs, which could be deductible as business expenses.

Blockchain technology's decentralized and pseudonymous nature poses significant challenges for tax authorities in tracking and regulating cryptocurrency transactions. Unlike traditional financial systems, cryptocurrency transactions are not directly linked to individuals' identities, making it difficult for tax authorities to identify taxpayers engaged in cryptocurrency activities. As a result, taxpayers may be tempted to underreport or omit cryptocurrency transactions, leading to potential tax evasion. Cryptocurrency transactions conducted across international borders can further complicate tax reporting and compliance. Taxpayers engaged in cross-border transactions must navigate the tax regulations of multiple countries, which may have differing tax treatment for cryptocurrencies. Additionally, taxpayers may be subject to foreign tax reporting requirements and potential double taxation issues.

Using cryptocurrencies to purchase goods and services can also have tax implications. In some jurisdictions, using cryptocurrencies for transactions is considered a taxable event, and taxpayers are required to compute and report the capital gains or losses resulting from the use of cryptocurrencies as payment. However, tracking the value of cryptocurrencies used in everyday transactions can be challenging, especially when their prices are subject to frequent fluctuations. Giving cryptocurrencies as gifts or making charitable donations in cryptocurrencies can also have tax consequences. In many jurisdictions, gifts of cryptocurrencies may be subject to gift tax if they exceed certain thresholds. Additionally, charitable donations in cryptocurrencies may be eligible for tax deductions, but specific rules and requirements must be met for the donations to qualify for tax benefits.

Given the complexities of cryptocurrency taxation, maintaining precise and detailed records of every cryptocurrency transactions is vital for tax compliance. Keeping track of the acquisition and disposal dates, the fair market value at the time of the transaction, and the purpose of each transaction can significantly simplify tax reporting and reduce the risk of errors or audits. As the cryptocurrency market continues to evolve, tax authorities are grappling with the need to develop clear and comprehensive guidelines for cryptocurrency taxation. The lack of uniformity in cryptocurrency tax regulations across jurisdictions creates uncertainty for taxpayers and may hinder the growth of the cryptocurrency industry. Clear and updated regulations are essential to provide taxpayers with a clear understanding of their tax obligations and to promote compliance.

Taxpayers engaged in cryptocurrency transactions may consider employing tax planning strategies to maximize their tax liabilities legally. These strategies may include tax loss harvesting, timing transactions to qualify for long-term capital gains tax rates, and optimizing deductions for business-related cryptocurrency activities. Tax professionals with expertise in cryptocurrency taxation can provide valuable guidance in developing effective tax planning strategies. In conclusion, the tax implications of cryptocurrency transactions present unique challenges for both taxpayers and tax authorities. The treatment of cryptocurrencies as property for tax purposes, capital gains tax, holding periods, crypto-to-crypto transactions, mining income, tax reporting challenges, international transactions, crypto payments, gift and donation tax, tax compliance, regulatory developments, and tax planning strategies are all critical aspects that taxpayers must consider in navigating the complexities of the digital economy.

Tax authorities must adapt their regulations as the cryptocurrency market matures to keep pace with technological advancements and changing market dynamics. Clarity in cryptocurrency tax regulations and effective enforcement measures are vital to promoting compliance and ensuring taxpayers meet their tax obligations. By understanding the tax implications and seeking professional advice, individuals and businesses can navigate cryptocurrency taxation's intricacies, ensuring compliance with tax laws and optimal financial planning in this dynamic and transformative digital age.

CHAPTER X

Diversifying Your Crypto Portfolio

Building a diversified portfolio

The cryptocurrency market has witnessed explosive growth over the past decade, attracting investors seeking to capitalize on the potential of this innovative asset class. As the market matures, investors become increasingly aware of the significance of building a diversified portfolio to manage risks and enhance returns.

Diversification is a basic principle of investment that involves spreading one's investments across different assets, industries, and geographic regions. Diversification means holding a mix of other cryptocurrencies rather than concentrating all investments in a single digital asset.

Diversification offers several advantages in the volatile cryptocurrency market. Firstly, it can help mitigate the impact of price fluctuations in any individual cryptocurrency. Cryptocurrencies are well-known for their extreme price volatility, and holding a diversified portfolio can help mitigate the overall risk exposure to the market's ups and downs. Additionally, a diversified portfolio can provide exposure to different blockchain projects and use cases, increasing the potential for capitalizing on various emerging trends and technologies within the cryptocurrency ecosystem.

Building a diversified cryptocurrency portfolio involves selecting a mix of cryptocurrencies with different characteristics and use cases. Major cryptocurrencies like Bitcoin (BTC) and Ethereum (ETH) are considered the blue-chip assets of the cryptocurrency market. They are more established, have higher liquidity, and generally have a lower risk profile than other cryptocurrencies. On the other hand, altcoins refer to all other cryptocurrencies besides Bitcoin. These include projects with unique features, niche use cases, and potentially higher growth prospects. Altcoins can offer diversification benefits as they may have different price movements than major cryptocurrencies. Stablecoins, a special category of cryptocurrencies pegged to stable assets like fiat currencies or commodities, aim to maintain a stable value and can act as a hedge against market volatility.

When building a diversified cryptocurrency portfolio, investors need to conduct a profound research and due diligence on each cryptocurrency they plan to include. Factors to consider include the project's underlying technology, team, community support, market capitalization, liquidity, and potential for adoption. Understanding the risks and potential of each cryptocurrency is crucial in making informed investment decisions.

Determining the allocation of funds across different cryptocurrencies is another critical aspect of building a diversified portfolio. The allocation strategy should align with the investor's risk tolerance, investment goals, and time horizon. A greater risk tolerance may lead some investors to adopt a more aggressive strategy, allocating a sizeable portion of their capital to altcoins with greater growth potential, while more cautious investors may allocate a sizeable portion of their capital to major cryptocurrencies and stablecoins.

A well-diversified cryptocurrency portfolio requires ongoing monitoring and periodic rebalancing. Rebalancing entails adjusting the allocation of funds to maintain the desired level of diversification. For example, if the value of a particular cryptocurrency significantly increases, it may lead to an overweight position in the portfolio. Rebalancing helps return the portfolio to the desired asset allocation and manage risk effectively.

Dollar-cost averaging, or DCA is a strategy in which investors regularly invest a fixed amount of money in their portfolio, regardless of the cryptocurrency's price. DCA can be an effective method to reduce the influence of market volatility on investment returns and can be especially valuable for investors who want to build a long-term diversified cryptocurrency portfolio gradually.

Building a diversified portfolio in cryptocurrency is not without its challenges and risks. The cryptocurrency market is still relatively young and can be highly speculative. Investors may face liquidity issues, price manipulation, and the risk of investing in projects that fail to deliver on their promises. Moreover, regulatory uncertainties and market sentiment can significantly impact cryptocurrency prices, increasing portfolio volatility.

The investment horizon is an essential consideration when building a diversified cryptocurrency portfolio. Long-term investors may adopt a buy-and-hold strategy, focusing on assets with solid fundamentals and long-term potential. On the other hand, short-term traders may take advantage of price movements and market trends to achieve more frequent gains. The investment approach should align with the investor's financial goals and risk tolerance.

Risk management is crucial to investing in cryptocurrency, especially given the market's inherent volatility. Setting clear risk management strategies, such as implementing stop-loss orders or position-sizing techniques, can help protect the portfolio from significant losses during market downturns.

In the fast-paced cryptocurrency market, staying informed and educated is essential. Market conditions, technology developments, and regulatory changes can significantly impact cryptocurrency prices. Regularly monitoring industry news and updates can help investors make informed decisions and adjust their portfolio strategies accordingly.

In conclusion, building a diversified portfolio in cryptocurrency is a prudent approach to navigating the inherent risks and opportunities in this emerging asset class. Diversification can help mitigate the effect of price fluctuations, increase exposure to different cryptocurrencies and use cases, and enhance the potential for long-term returns. However, investors must conduct thorough research, assess risk and potential, and implement effective risk management strategies to build a robust and well-balanced cryptocurrency portfolio. As the cryptocurrency market continues to evolve, disciplined and informed investors can position themselves to maximize the potential of this transformative digital asset class while managing risks responsibly.

Evaluating risk and potential returns

The world of cryptocurrency has captured the attention of investors worldwide, promising exciting opportunities and potential for substantial returns. However, along with the allure of rapid growth comes inherent risk. This section delves into the complexities of evaluating risk and potential returns in the cryptocurrency market, highlighting the unique challenges and methodologies investors must consider to navigate this digital frontier's volatility successfully.

Cryptocurrencies are well-known for their extreme price volatility, often experiencing significant price fluctuations within short timeframes. This inherent risk stems from various factors, including market sentiment, regulatory developments, technological advancements, and macroeconomic trends. The lack of intrinsic value and limited regulatory oversight also contribute to the high level of uncertainty surrounding cryptocurrencies. As a result, investors must approach the evaluation of risk in cryptocurrency with caution and diligence.

Numerous factors influence the risk profile of cryptocurrencies. Market sentiment plays a crucial role, making the market susceptible to news, rumors, and social media trends. Regulatory actions or announcements by governments and financial institutions can significantly impact cryptocurrency prices, increasing volatility. Technological vulnerabilities, security breaches, and potential network forks can also expose cryptocurrencies to significant risk.

Volatility is a key indicator of risk in the cryptocurrency market. Cryptocurrencies with high volatility are more susceptible to large price swings, which can result in substantial gains or losses for investors. While high volatility can present opportunities for significant returns, it also amplifies the potential for losses, making risk assessment a critical component of investment decisions.

Evaluating historical performance is a common approach to assessing risk and potential returns in the cryptocurrency market. By examining past price movements and performance metrics, investors can gain insights into the asset's volatility, market trends, and growth potential. However, it is essential to recognize that historical performance does not indicate future results, particularly in cryptocurrencies' rapidly evolving and speculative nature.

Fundamental analysis involves evaluating the underlying factors that influence a cryptocurrency's value and potential growth. Key elements of fundamental analysis include assessing the technology, use case, team, community support, and potential for mass adoption. Investors conduct due diligence on blockchain projects to identify strong fundamentals and promising projects with the potential for long-term growth.

To identify patterns and trends, technical analysis studies past market data, primarily price and trading volume. Technical analysts use charts, indicators, and mathematical models to predict future price movements. While technical analysis can offer helpful insights into market sentiment and potential price trends, it also has its limitations, particularly in the cryptocurrency market, where external factors can heavily influence price movements.

Effective risk management is crucial for investors in the cryptocurrency market. As mentioned in the previous section, diversification is a primary risk management strategy. By spreading investments over different cryptocurrencies and asset classes, investors can mitigate their exposure to individual asset risks. Additionally, setting clear stop-loss levels and position-sizing techniques can help protect investments from significant losses during market downturns.

Assessing potential returns in the cryptocurrency market requires a balanced approach considering risk and opportunity. High volatility and the potential for rapid growth make cryptocurrencies attractive to investors seeking substantial returns. However, the speculative nature of the market also increases the risk of significant losses. Investors must carefully consider their risk tolerance, investment horizon, and financial goals when evaluating the potential for returns in the cryptocurrency market.

With thousands of cryptocurrencies available in the market, investors need to evaluate the legitimacy and credibility of blockchain projects. Many projects lack proper development, solid use cases, or a committed team, making them susceptible to failure or fraudulent activities. Investors must conduct an in-depth research and due diligence to identify projects with real-world potential and robust fundamentals.

The regulatory environment is significant in shaping risk and potential returns in the cryptocurrency market. Different countries have varying stances on cryptocurrency regulation, and regulatory actions can significantly impact market sentiment and investment decisions. Investors must stay informed about regulatory developments and consider the potential risks of the evolving regulatory landscape.

Investing in cryptocurrencies can evoke strong emotions, including fear of missing out (FOMO) and fear of loss (FOL). These emotional responses can influence investment decisions and lead to impulsive actions.

Rational evaluation of risk and potential returns requires discipline and managing emotions effectively.

In conclusion, evaluating risk and potential returns in the cryptocurrency market is a multifaceted and dynamic process. Investors must approach this new asset class with a clear understanding of its risks and challenges. While high volatility and speculative nature can lead to substantial gains, they also amplify the potential for losses. By conducting thorough research, applying sound risk management strategies, and assessing projects based on solid fundamentals, investors can navigate the complexities of the cryptocurrency market and make informed investment decisions. As the market continues to evolve, knowledgeable and disciplined investors can harness the potential of this digital frontier while effectively managing risk.

Asset allocation strategies

A fundamental investment strategy that divides an investment portfolio over different asset classes, such as stocks, bonds, real estate, and cash is known as asset allocation. In cryptocurrency, asset allocation refers to diversifying investments across different digital assets to manage risk and optimize returns.

The cryptocurrency market is well-known by its high volatility and unpredictable price movements. By allocating investments across a diverse range of cryptocurrencies, investors can reduce exposure to individual asset risks and potentially capitalize on various market trends and emerging technologies.

Investors can employ several asset allocation strategies in the cryptocurrency market. A conservative allocation strategy involves allocating more of the portfolio to stable and well-established cryptocurrencies like Bitcoin (BTC) and Ethereum (ETH). On the other end of the spectrum, an aggressive allocation strategy involves allocating a more significant portion of the portfolio to riskier and more volatile cryptocurrencies, often called altcoins. The balanced allocation strategy strikes a middle ground between conservative and aggressive approaches. Investors following this strategy aim to achieve a combination of stable growth and potential high returns by diversifying their portfolio across a mix of major cryptocurrencies and promising altcoins.

Diversification is a central tenet of asset allocation in cryptocurrency. Given the vast array of cryptocurrencies available, investors can create a diversified portfolio by selecting a mix of assets with different risk profiles, market capitalizations, and use cases. Diversification helps spread risk, reducing the impact of price fluctuations in any individual asset.

Risk management is a critical aspect of asset allocation in cryptocurrency. Setting clear risk management strategies, such as implementing stop-loss orders and position-sizing techniques, can help protect the portfolio from significant losses during market downturns.

Rebalancing is the procedure of adjusting the allocation of assets in the portfolio to maintain the desired level of diversification. Regularly rebalancing the cryptocurrency portfolio can ensure that it aligns with the investor's risk tolerance and investment goals.

Investment time horizon and goals are crucial in determining the appropriate asset allocation strategy. Long-term investors with a higher risk tolerance may opt for a more aggressive allocation, while those with a shorter time horizon or reduced risk tolerance may prefer a conservative or balanced approach.

Due diligence is essential when evaluating potential cryptocurrencies for inclusion in the portfolio. Fundamental analysis helps investors assess the technology, use case, team, community support, and potential for cryptocurrency adoption. A thorough evaluation of projects can increase the likelihood of making informed investment decisions.

Bitcoin often serves as a core asset in cryptocurrency portfolios. As the first and most popular cryptocurrency, Bitcoin is seen as a store of value and a hedge against market volatility. Many investors consider Bitcoin as a foundational component of their cryptocurrency portfolio due to its historical performance and widespread recognition.

Monitoring market trends and industry developments is crucial in the cryptocurrency market. Various factors, including technological advancements, regulatory changes, macroeconomic trends, and shifts in investor sentiment influence the market. Staying informed about market trends can help investors adjust their asset allocation strategy accordingly.

The cryptocurrency market is dynamic and ever-evolving. New cryptocurrencies and projects emerge regularly, while others may fade into obscurity. Investors must be adaptable and open to adjusting their asset allocation strategy based on market conditions and new opportunities.

While diversification is essential, overexposure to the cryptocurrency market can also pose risks. Some investors may become overly concentrated in the digital asset space, neglecting the benefits of diversifying across traditional asset classes. Maintaining a balanced portfolio that includes a mix of cryptocurrencies and other investments can help mitigate risks.

In conclusion, developing a sound asset allocation strategy is essential for investors looking to venture into the cryptocurrency market. Diversification, risk management, and time horizon are key considerations that can help investors balance risk and return effectively. While the cryptocurrency market offers exciting opportunities, it also presents unique challenges, emphasizing the significance of conducting thorough research and due diligence prior making investment decisions. By employing prudent asset allocation strategies, investors can navigate the volatile digital asset space and position themselves for cryptocurrencies' potential growth and transformative power in the global financial landscape.

CHAPTER XI

Day Trading vs. Long-Term Holding

Day trading cryptocurrencies

Day trading cryptocurrencies have gained immense popularity in recent years, driven by the allure of rapid profits and the excitement of navigating the volatile digital asset market. This fast-paced trading strategy involves buying and selling financial instruments within the same day, aiming to profit from short-term price movements. The cryptocurrency market operates 24/7, providing ample trading opportunities at any time of the day or night. Moreover, the market's high volatility creates frequent price swings, presenting potential opportunities for substantial profits in a short period.

Day traders in the cryptocurrency market employ various strategies to execute their trades successfully. With the scalping method, traders make several fast transactions during the day in an attempt to profit from little price swings. Momentum traders, on the other hand, look for cryptocurrencies showing strong upward or downward momentum and aim to ride the trend. Breakout traders focus on significant price levels, such as support or resistance, and enter a trade when the price breaks out of those levels. Contrarian traders take positions opposite to the prevailing market sentiment, hoping to profit from potential market reversals.

Despite the allure of day trading in cryptocurrencies, it comes with substantial risks. The market's high volatility can lead to significant losses if not managed properly. Effective risk management is crucial for day traders to protect their capital and survive in the highly competitive trading environment. Setting strict stop-loss orders and determining appropriate position sizes relative to the trader's overall capital are essential risk management techniques.

Day trading cryptocurrencies can be mentally demanding. The fast-paced nature of the market requires quick decision-making and the ability to control emotions during periods of intense price fluctuations. Fear of missing out (FOMO) and fear of loss (FOL) are common emotional responses that can influence trading decisions and lead to impulsive actions. Maintaining discipline and following a well-defined trading plan can help day traders manage psychological challenges and avoid making emotional-based decisions.

Day traders use technical analysis to analyze price charts and identify potential entry and exit points. Various technical indicators and chart patterns help traders make knowledgeable decisions based on past price movements and market trends. However, it is essential to recognize that technical analysis has limitations, and the cryptocurrency market can be influenced by external elements, such as news and regulatory announcements, which may not be reflected in price charts.

Liquidity is a critical factor in day trading cryptocurrencies. Highly liquid assets allow traders to enter and exit positions quickly at desired price levels. Lower liquidity can result in slippage, where trades are executed at a different price than intended, impacting potential profits. Moreover, execution speed is crucial in day trading, as price movements can be swift and volatile.

Traders often rely on advanced trading platforms and low-latency connections to ensure fast order execution.

Selecting a reliable and efficient trading platform is essential for day traders. The platform should offer real-time data, advanced charting tools, fast execution, and user-friendly interfaces. Additionally, traders must consider security measures, as they need to deposit funds and execute trades on these platforms.

Day trading can be cost-intensive due to fees and costs associated with trading. These may include trading fees, exchange fees, withdrawal fees, and spreads. Traders must carefully evaluate these costs to ensure they do not significantly erode potential profits.

Day trading cryptocurrencies is subject to different regulatory frameworks worldwide. Traders should know the legal requirements and tax implications in their respective jurisdictions. The regulatory landscape can impact trading activities, and compliance is crucial to avoid legal issues.

The cryptocurrency market is still relatively young and less regulated than traditional financial markets. This lack of oversight can lead to market manipulation and price manipulation schemes. Traders must exercise caution and stay vigilant to avoid falling victim to such schemes.

In conclusion, day trading cryptocurrencies can be a thrilling and potentially lucrative endeavor for traders with the necessary skills, knowledge, and discipline. However, it is not without its challenges and risks. Traders must be prepared to deal with the market's high volatility, manage risk effectively, and navigate the psychological challenges of intraday trading. Technical analysis, risk management strategies, and a well-defined trading plan are essential tools for day traders aiming to capitalize on the fast-paced world of cryptocurrency trading. As the cryptocurrency market continues to evolve, informed and skilled day traders can seize opportunities and contribute to the ongoing growth and maturity of this dynamic digital asset space.

The benefits of long-term holding

Cryptocurrencies have emerged as a compelling asset class, attracting investors with their potential for exponential gains and technological innovation. While day trading and short-term speculation have their allure, long-term holding, also known as "HODLing" in the crypto community, has gained popularity as a strategic approach to maximizing returns and capitalizing on the transformative potential of digital assets.

Long-term holding allows investors to embrace the volatility inherent in the cryptocurrency market. Cryptocurrencies are well-known for their extreme price swings, making short-term trading challenging. By holding through market cycles and fluctuations, long-term investors can benefit from the overall growth trajectory of the cryptocurrency market.

The cryptocurrency space is continually evolving, with advancements in blockchain technology, DeFi (Decentralized Finance), and NFTs (Non-Fungible Tokens) reshaping the industry. Long-term holding allows investors to capitalize on these technological developments and their probable impact on the value of cryptocurrencies. Patience can be rewarding, as innovative projects and real-world use cases emerge, potentially driving long-term value appreciation.

Unlike short-term traders, long-term investors are more inclined to avoid emotional decision-making. Short-term trading often involves quick decision-making, driven by market sentiment and emotional responses to price fluctuations. These impulsive decisions can lead to losses and missed opportunities. Long-term holding encourages a more rational and patient approach, helping investors focus on the underlying fundamentals of their chosen assets.

Frequent trading incurs transaction costs, including exchange fees, spread, and other expenses, which can eat into potential profits. Moreover, depending on the investor's jurisdiction, short-term trading can trigger higher capital gains taxes. Long-term holding offers tax advantages in some regions, where capital gains taxes are lower for assets held for more extended periods, further maximizing potential returns.

The cryptocurrency market is still in its early stages, with ongoing regulatory developments and institutional interest influencing its growth. Long-term holding positions investors to benefit from the market's maturation and increased adoption. As institutional adoption grows, the entry of traditional financial players could potentially drive higher demand and price appreciation in the long term.

The cryptocurrency market experiences cyclical downturns, known as bear markets, where prices decline significantly. Short-term traders may face challenges in navigating these periods, while long-term investors can weather the storms and potentially capitalize on the subsequent bull markets. Holding through bear markets allows investors to ride out temporary price declines and participate in the subsequent market recovery.

Long-term holding often requires thorough research and conviction in the chosen projects. Investors can be more resilient during market fluctuations by investing in cryptocurrencies with a strong belief in their potential. Strong convictions can help long-term holders stay committed to their investment thesis, even when facing short-term challenges.

Long-term holding can lead to compounding gains over time. As cryptocurrencies appreciate in value, the profits can be reinvested or compounded, leading to exponential growth in the investment. This compounding effect can be potent in the cryptocurrency market due to its higher volatility than traditional asset classes.

Long-term holding allows investors to build a diversified cryptocurrency portfolio. By holding multiple assets with varying risk profiles, investors can spread risk and reduce exposure to any asset's price fluctuations. Diversification is a critical risk management strategy that can enhance portfolio stability and resilience.

Cryptocurrencies embody the principles of decentralization, empowering individuals to control their financial assets without relying on centralized intermediaries. Long-term holding supports the decentralization narrative by reducing the reliance on short-term speculative trading that may lead to excessive market manipulation and volatility.

The cryptocurrency space is at the forefront of financial innovation and disruption. Long-term investors are vital in supporting and financing these innovative projects and initiatives. By holding through the development stages, investors contribute to the growth and success of promising blockchain projects, enabling transformative change in various industries.

In conclusion, long-term holding in cryptocurrencies presents a strategic investment approach that offers numerous benefits over short-term trading. By embracing volatility, capitalizing on technological advancements, and avoiding emotional decision-making, long-term investors can position themselves for potential long-term gains. Moreover, long-term holding allows investors to weather market downturns, benefit from compounding gains, and contribute to the growth and decentralization of the cryptocurrency space. While long-term holding requires patience and strong convictions, it aligns with the ethos of cryptocurrencies, empowering individuals to have control over their financial future. As the cryptocurrency market matures and gains broader acceptance, long-term investors can play a crucial role in shaping the future of finance and unlocking the transformative potential of digital assets.

Balancing trading and investing

The cryptocurrency market has become a dynamic and lucrative arena, attracting traders seeking short-term profits and investors looking to capitalize on long-term growth potential. The strategies of trading and investing in cryptocurrencies serve distinct purposes, each with unique advantages and risks. However, finding the right balance between trading and investing is essential for maximizing gains and managing risk effectively.

Trading cryptocurrencies can be alluring due to its potential for quick profits. The crypto market's high volatility presents frequent price swings, creating opportunities for traders to capitalize on upward and downward movements. Moreover, the market's 24/7 operation allows traders to execute trades anytime, offering flexibility and continuous trading opportunities.

On the other hand, investing in cryptocurrencies offers several advantages, particularly for those who believe in the long-term potential of blockchain technology and digital assets. By holding through market cycles, investors can benefit from the overall market growth, technological advancements, and widespread adoption of cryptocurrencies. Investing also allows individuals to support promising projects and decentralized initiatives, contributing to the transformation of various industries.

Both trading and investing in cryptocurrencies come with their challenges. Trading requires constant monitoring of the market, quick decision-making, and a deep understanding of technical analysis. The fast-paced nature of trading can lead to emotional decision-making, increasing the risk of losses. While less intensive, investing requires patience and conviction in the chosen projects. The cryptocurrency market's volatility can test investors' resolve during bear markets, and holding through downturns may be mentally challenging.

The key to balancing trading and investing lies in recognizing the strengths and limitations of each approach and aligning them with personal financial goals and risk tolerance. Developing a well-defined trading plan is crucial for those engaged in short-term trading. This plan should outline risk management strategies, including setting stop-loss orders to limit potential losses. Additionally, traders should carefully select their trade assets, considering liquidity, volatility, and market sentiment.

On the other hand, investors should conduct thorough research on the projects they wish to support. Understanding a cryptocurrency's technology, team, community, and real-world use cases can provide valuable insights into its long-term potential. Patience is key for investors, as it allows them to ride out market cycles and avoid making rapid decisions based on short- term price movements.

A hybrid approach combining trading and investing elements is dollar-cost averaging (DCA). DCA involves regularly investing a fixed amount of money, regardless of the cryptocurrency's current price. This strategy allows investors to mitigate the impact of market volatility by buying more when prices are low and less when prices are high. DCA is particularly suited for investors who want to enter the market gradually and build a long-term position in cryptocurrencies.

Regardless of the chosen approach, building a diversified cryptocurrency portfolio is crucial for managing risk effectively. A diversified portfolio includes a mix of cryptocurrencies with varying risk profiles and growth potentials. This approach helps spread risk and reduces the impact of any single asset's price fluctuations on the overall portfolio.

In the ever-changing cryptocurrency landscape, staying informed is paramount. Both traders and investors must keep abreast of industry news, regulatory developments, technological advancements, and market trends. Being well-informed allows market participants to make educated decisions and adapt their strategies accordingly. Evaluating personal risk tolerance is an essential factor in balancing trading and investing in cryptocurrencies. Different individuals have varying risk tolerance levels, so aligning trading and investment strategies is crucial. High-risk tolerance individuals may opt for more aggressive trading strategies, while those with lower risk tolerance may lean towards long-term investing.

In conclusion, balancing trading and investing in cryptocurrencies is an art that requires understanding one's financial goals, risk tolerance, and time horizon. Trading offers potential for short-term profits but demands expertise, time commitment, and emotional discipline. Conversely, investing focuses on long-term growth and requires patience, strong convictions, and a belief in the transformative power of digital assets.

A hybrid approach, such as dollar-cost averaging, can provide the benefits of both trading and investing, allowing investors to gradually build a position in the market while mitigating the impact of market volatility. Regardless of the chosen approach, building a diversified portfolio, staying informed, and evaluating personal risk tolerance are essential for success in cryptocurrencies' dynamic and ever-evolving world. Finding the right balance between trading and investing is a strategic approach that enables individuals to maximize gains, navigate market fluctuations, and participate in the ongoing transformation of the financial landscape driven by the growing adoption of cryptocurrencies.

CHAPTER XII

Identifying and Avoiding Scams

Common cryptocurrency scams

Cryptocurrencies' rapid rise has brought numerous opportunities for investors and traders. However, the cryptocurrency market is rife with scams and fraudulent schemes alongside legitimate projects and platforms. These scams target unsuspecting individuals, aiming to steal their hard-earned money or sensitive information. This section delves into the common cryptocurrency scams in the digital asset space. By understanding these threats, investors can better safeguard their investments and participate in the cryptocurrency market more securely.

Ponzi schemes and pyramid schemes are among the oldest and most prevalent scams in the financial world. In the context of cryptocurrencies, they operate by promising high returns on investments to participants. These schemes create the appearance of profitability by using the money of new investors to pay the returns that were promised to previous investors. Eventually, the scheme collapses when it becomes unsustainable, leaving the majority of participants with significant losses.

Fake ICOs (Initial Coin Offerings) have also proliferated in cryptocurrency. Scammers set up fake ICO websites, promising revolutionary projects and high returns to investors. Once they have collected enough funds, they disappear, leaving investors with worthless tokens.

Phishing attacks are a common cybercrime technique used to trick individuals into disclosing their sensitive information, such as passwords, private keys, and login credentials. In the context of cryptocurrencies, scammers create fake websites or send fraudulent emails that mimic legitimate cryptocurrency platforms or exchanges.

Fake exchanges and trading platforms are also prevalent in the crypto world. Scammers often create fake cryptocurrency exchanges that appear legitimate to lure in users. These platforms may offer attractive trading fees, bonus incentives, and promising investment opportunities. However, once users deposit their funds, they may find withdrawing or facing technical issues challenging.

Pump and dump schemes involve artificially inflating the price of a cryptocurrency through misleading information and hype. Scammers promote a particular cryptocurrency, urging others to buy and inflate its price. Once the price reaches a certain level, the scammers sell their holdings at a profit, causing the price to plummet. Unsuspecting investors who bought at the peak experience substantial losses.

Social media impersonations are another common tactic used by scammers. They often impersonate well-known figures, celebrities, or cryptocurrency influencers to deceive users. They may create fake accounts and use the impersonated figure's name and image to endorse fraudulent projects or investment opportunities.

Malware and ransomware attacks are malicious software programs that infiltrate users' devices and compromise their data or cryptocurrency wallets. Scammers may use malware to steal private keys, passwords, or other sensitive information. Ransomware attacks, on the other hand, encrypt users' files or data and demand a ransom in cryptocurrency to release the decryption key.

Fake wallets are another way scammers attempt to steal cryptocurrency. Cryptocurrency wallet applications are essential for securely storing digital assets. However, scammers create fake wallet applications and distribute them through unofficial channels or app stores. Unsuspecting users who download these fake wallets may expose their private keys and lose their cryptocurrencies.

Investment and trading signal groups on platforms like Telegram can also be fraudulent. Some of these groups may be operated by scammers who claim to offer insider information or trading signals that promise substantial profits. However, they may be manipulating market sentiment to trick users into making specific trades that benefit the scammers.

Celebrity endorsement scams involve scammers using fake celebrity endorsements to promote fraudulent cryptocurrency schemes. They fabricate celebrity quotes or testimonials, claiming they have invested in a particular cryptocurrency project. Such endorsements can mislead individuals into trusting the project's legitimacy when, in fact, the celebrity has no association with it.

In conclusion, the rise in the adoption of cryptocurrencies is accompanied by an increase in the number of fraud and scams involving digital assets. Investors and users must be cautious when engaging with cryptocurrency projects, platforms, or investment opportunities. To safeguard investments, individuals should conduct thorough research, verify the legitimacy of projects and platforms, and avoid participating in suspicious ventures. Additionally, implementing robust security measures, such as using hardware wallets, enabling two-factor authentication, and being cautious of unsolicited communications, can go a long way in protecting assets from scammers. By being informed and proactive, individuals can minimize the risks associated with common cryptocurrency scams and participate in the cryptocurrency market more securely.

Tips for staying safe in the crypto space

The first and most crucial step in staying safe in the crypto space is education. Understanding how cryptocurrencies work, the underlying blockchain technology, and the various security measures available is essential. Invest time in researching reputable sources, tutorials, and official documentation from blockchain projects and exchanges. Being well-informed will empower you to make better decisions, recognize potential threats, and protect yourself from scams.

Choosing a cryptocurrency wallet can significantly impact the safety of your digital assets. Use wallets from reputable providers that offer robust security features. Since hardware wallets store private keys offline and are therefore less vulnerable to hacking attempts, they are frequently regarded as the most secure alternative. Additionally, enable two-factor authentication (2FA) on all your wallets and accounts to add an extra layer of security.

Phishing attacks remain one of the most common cyber threats in crypto. Scammers use fake websites, emails, or messages that mimic legitimate platforms to trick users into revealing their sensitive information. Always double-check the URLs of websites and avoid clicking on suspicious links. Be cautious of unsolicited communications and never share your private keys or passwords with anyone.

Ensure that all your devices, including computers and smartphones, have the latest operating system and security updates installed. Regularly update your cryptocurrency wallet software and any other applications related to managing your digital assets. Outdated software can contain vulnerabilities that hackers may exploit to gain unauthorized access to your funds.

The strength of your passwords and PINs is critical in securing your crypto assets. Avoid using easily guessable combinations and opt for complex passwords that entail a mix of uppercase and lowercase letters, numbers, and special characters. Refrain from reusing passwords across different platforms to prevent the risk of multiple accounts being compromised if one is breached.

Investing in cryptocurrencies involves risk, and it is essential to practice risk management to protect your capital. Don't invest all of the funds you have in one cryptocurrency; instead, just invest money you can afford to lose. To mitigate risk and lower the impact of market changes, diversify your investments among a variety of assets.

Utilizing public Wi-Fi networks to access cryptocurrency wallets or exchange accounts carries significant risks due to their susceptibility to security breaches. Refrain from using public Wi-Fi to access sensitive data or conduct transactions. Use a private, secure network instead, or, for even more security, think about utilizing a virtual private network (VPN).

Always double-check the wallet addresses to ensure accuracy when sending or receiving cryptocurrency.

Cryptocurrency transactions are irreversible, and sending money to the wrong address may lead to permanent loss. Cross-verify the addresses using multiple sources, such as scanning QR codes or copying and pasting the addresses.

The crypto space is not immune to investment scams and fraudulent schemes. Exercise caution when encountering investment opportunities that promise unrealistically high returns or use aggressive marketing tactics. Conduct thorough research on the projects and platforms before investing, and be skeptical of offers that seem too good to be true.

Regularly backup your cryptocurrency wallet and store the backup in a secure and offline location. This precaution ensures you can recover your funds in case of hardware failures, lost devices, or accidental data loss. Test the backup recovery process to ensure its effectiveness.

The crypto space is constantly evolving, and new security threats may emerge. Stay updated on the most current security practices and be aware of recent security breaches or vulnerabilities. Being informed will enable you to protect your assets from potential threats promptly.

Multi-signature wallets necessitate multiple private keys to authorize transactions, adding an extra layer of security. Consider using multi-signature wallets for significant transactions or long-term holdings, as they can significantly reduce the risk of unauthorized access to your funds.

While some cryptocurrency exchanges offer custodial services, meaning they hold your funds on your behalf, consider self-custodying your assets. Self-custody gives you complete control over your private keys and reduces the risk of compromised funds through exchange hacks or insider theft.

Engaging with the cryptocurrency community can provide valuable insights and inform you about potential scams or security risks. Participate in online forums, social media groups, and official community channels to share knowledge and stay updated on the latest developments.

If you encounter suspicious activities, scams, or fraudulent schemes in crypto, report them to the relevant authorities or platforms. Reporting such incidents protects you and helps protect others in the community from falling victim to similar scams.

In conclusion, navigating the crypto space safely requires a combination of vigilance, education, and adopting best security practices. By staying informed, using secure wallets, practicing risk management, and being cautious of potential threats, you can safeguard your digital assets and enjoy the benefits of engaging in the exciting world of cryptocurrencies. Remember that securing your crypto holdings is an ongoing process, and staying proactive is crucial in safeguarding your investments in this rapidly evolving landscape.

CHAPTER XIII

The Future of Cryptocurrencies

Emerging trends and technologies

The cryptocurrency space is an ever-evolving landscape, continually witnessing the emergence of new trends and technologies that shape the future of digital assets. From the early days of Bitcoin's creation to the explosion of decentralized finance (DeFi) and non-fungible tokens (NFTs), the crypto industry has experienced rapid developments and paradigm shifts.

Decentralized Finance, or DeFi, has emerged as a disruptive force in crypto, redefining traditional financial systems through decentralized protocols and applications. DeFi platforms enable users to access various financial services, including lending, borrowing, trading, and yield farming, without intermediaries like banks.

Non-Fungible Tokens, or NFTs, have become a major trend in the crypto space, revolutionizing digital ownership and intellectual property rights. NFTs are unique digital assets representing ownership of a specific item, artwork, or digital collectible on the blockchain. They leverage blockchain technology to certify authenticity, provenance, and scarcity, making them highly sought after by artists, creators, and collectors. Central Bank Digital Currencies (CBDCs) have emerged as a potential evolution of traditional fiat currencies in the digital age. CBDCs are digital representations of a nation's fiat currency issued and regulated by its central bank. These digital currencies aim to enhance financial inclusivity, streamline cross-border payments, and provide a more efficient and secure means of conducting transactions.

Scalability remains a major challenge for many blockchain networks, leading to congestion and high transaction fees during peak periods. Layer 2 scaling solutions aim to address these issues by building additional layers on top of existing blockchains to process transactions off-chain or more efficiently.

The interoperability of different blockchain networks has become a pressing need in crypto. As multiple blockchains with unique features and functionalities emerge, the ability to seamlessly transfer assets and data across different networks becomes essential for the ecosystem's growth.

Decentralized Autonomous Organizations (DAOs) represent a novel approach to governance and decision-making within the crypto space. DAOs are organizations that operate through smart contracts on the blockchain, allowing stakeholders to participate in decision-making and governance processes through voting mechanisms. Privacy remains a crucial aspect of crypto, mainly as public blockchains record all transactions on an immutable ledger. Privacy-focused technologies, such as zero-knowledge proofs and cryptographic techniques like zk-SNARKs, enable users to transact privately without revealing sensitive information on the blockchain.

The impact in environment of cryptocurrency mining has been a growing concern within the crypto community and beyond. As the energy consumption of some proof-of-work (PoW) blockchains raises environmental questions, emerging trends focus on developing sustainable consensus mechanisms.

Institutional adoption of cryptocurrencies and blockchain technology has been gaining momentum, with major companies, financial institutions, and even governments exploring blockchain applications and digital asset investments. As institutional interest grows, regulatory clarity becomes essential to provide businesses and investors with a stable and transparent environment.

The crypto space continues to witness dynamic shifts with the emergence of new trends and technologies. DeFi and NFTs have redefined financial services and digital ownership, while CBDCs offer a potential future for sovereign digital currencies. Layer 2 scaling solutions, interoperability efforts, and DAOs address scalability, cross-chain communication, and decentralized governance challenges.

Privacy, security, environmental sustainability, and regulatory clarity remain crucial aspects for the sustainable growth of the crypto industry. As the landscape evolves, continuous innovation, responsible development, and collaboration between stakeholders will shape the crypto space's future and blockchain technology's transformative impact on various industries.

Potential challenges and opportunities

The crypto space has grown exponentially over the past decade, transforming the financial landscape and offering numerous opportunities for innovation and disruption. As cryptocurrencies and blockchain technology continue gaining traction, they present various potential challenges and opportunities stakeholders must navigate.

One of the most prominent challenges facing the crypto space is regulatory uncertainty. Different countries and jurisdictions have taken varying approaches to cryptocurrency regulation, leading to a fragmented and often confusing legal landscape. Some countries have included cryptocurrencies and blockchain technology, providing clear frameworks and regulations, while others have adopted more cautious or restrictive stances. The lack of consistent and comprehensive regulation can hinder innovation, create compliance burdens for businesses, and potentially expose users to fraudulent schemes. However, establishing clear and balanced regulatory frameworks presents an opportunity for the crypto space to gain mainstream acceptance and foster responsible growth.

Security remains a top concern in the crypto space. While blockchain technology offers robust security features, cryptocurrency users are still vulnerable to hacks, phishing attacks, and scams. High-profile incidents of exchange hacks and stolen funds have highlighted the requirement for more robust security measures. Additionally, the risk of smart contract vulnerabilities and bugs in decentralized applications (dApps) threatens user funds and data. Investing in robust security protocols, adopting best practices, and promoting cybersecurity awareness can mitigate these risks and bolster confidence in the crypto ecosystem.

Cryptocurrencies are well-known for their extreme price volatility, which can lead to significant gains but also substantial losses for investors and traders. Various factors, including market sentiment, regulatory news, and macroeconomic events, influence price fluctuations. While volatility attracts speculative traders and investors seeking high returns, it also poses risks to those unprepared for sudden market swings. Implementing risk management strategies and understanding the underlying factors that drive volatility can help stakeholders navigate this aspect of the crypto space.

As adoption of cryptocurrencies grows, scalability becomes a critical challenge. Some blockchain networks, like the Bitcoin and Ethereum, face transaction throughput and processing capacity limitations, resulting in high transaction costs and network congestion at peak hours. Scalability solutions, such as layer 2 protocols and blockchain sharding, aim to address these issues and enhance network efficiency. Overcoming scalability challenges is essential for enabling cryptocurrencies to be viable alternatives to traditional payment systems.

Financial inclusion can be facilitated by cryptocurrencies, especially in areas where conventional banking services are scarce. Unbanked and underbanked people may take part in the global economy by having access to financial services through digital assets. However, challenges related to digital literacy, infrastructure, and regulatory barriers must be addressed to ensure that cryptocurrencies can truly empower the underserved populations.

Interoperability is a critical opportunity for the crypto space. As multiple blockchain networks with different protocols and functionalities emerge, the ability to seamlessly transfer assets and data between them becomes crucial for the growth of the ecosystem. Cross-chain communication protocols and decentralized bridges aim to foster collaboration between diverse blockchain networks, promoting innovation and expanding the possibilities for decentralized applications.

Institutional investors' increasing adoption of cryptocurrencies presents a significant opportunity for the crypto space. Institutions, including hedge funds, asset managers, and pension funds, have started to allocate funds to digital assets as part of their investment portfolios. This institutional interest can increase liquidity, price stability, and broader market acceptance. However, concerns over market manipulation and institutional investments' impact on market dynamics must be addressed to ensure fair and transparent markets.

Decentralized Finance (DeFi) has appeared as a revolutionary force in crypto, offering permissionless and inclusive financial services. DeFi protocols enable users to access lending, borrowing, trading, and yield farming without relying on traditional intermediaries. The democratization of finance through DeFi can empower individuals and small businesses, providing them with greater control over their financial activities. However, the rapid growth of DeFi also poses challenges related to security, regulatory compliance, and the potential for smart contract exploits.

The impact on the environment of cryptocurrency mining has become a contentious issue in the crypto space. Some proof-of-work (PoW) blockchains consume significant amounts of energy, resulting in concerns about their carbon footprint. PoW alternatives, such as proof-of-stake (PoS), offer more energy-efficient consensus mechanisms, and ongoing research aims to develop sustainable solutions for blockchain networks. Addressing the environmental impact of cryptocurrencies is a vital challenge that requires collaboration between the crypto community, researchers, and environmental experts.

Decentralized Autonomous Organizations (DAOs) present an opportunity to transform traditional governance models. DAOs operate through smart contracts, allowing stakeholders to participate in decision-making and resource allocation. Adopting decentralized governance structures can promote transparency, reduce bureaucracy, and foster community-driven initiatives. However, challenges related to participation, governance efficiency, and ensuring fair representation must be addressed to realize the full potential of DAOs.

In conclusion, the cryptocurrency space is a dynamic and rapidly evolving landscape, offering many opportunities and challenges. Regulatory uncertainty, security concerns, market volatility, and scalability issues represent significant challenges that stakeholders must overcome to enable the widespread adoption of cryptocurrencies and blockchain technology. On the other hand, financial inclusion, interoperability, institutional adoption, and DeFi present promising opportunities for transforming the global financial system and empowering individuals worldwide. Addressing these challenges and capitalizing on opportunities requires collaboration, innovation, and a commitment to responsible development within the crypto community and beyond. By navigating the path to a digital financial future with diligence and foresight, the crypto space can unlock its transformative potential and shape how we perceive and interact with money and assets in the future.

CONCLUSION

Recap of key concepts

Throughout this book, "Crypto Fundamentals: Unlocking the World of Cryptocurrencies - Essential Concepts and Strategies," we have embarked on a comprehensive journey to explore the fascinating world of cryptocurrencies, their underlying technologies, and the various strategies for navigating this ever-evolving landscape. As we conclude our exploration, we must recap the key concepts covered and reflect on the transformative potential of cryptocurrencies and blockchain technology.

In the initial sections of this book, we delved into the history of cryptocurrencies, tracing their origins back to the invention of Bitcoin by an anonymous entity known as Satoshi Nakamoto in 2008. The first and most popular cryptocurrency, Bitcoin, paved the way for a decentralized financial system, challenging the traditional centralized banking model. Since then, thousands of alternative cryptocurrencies, known as altcoins, have emerged, each with special features and use cases.

Defining cryptocurrencies and understanding how they work were fundamental building blocks in our journey. Cryptocurrencies are virtual or digital currencies that regulate the creation of new units and safeguard transactions through the use of cryptographic technology. They operate on decentralized networks, such as blockchain, which act as distributed ledgers to record all transactions transparently and immutably.

The significance of blockchain technology became apparent as we explored its applications beyond cryptocurrencies. Blockchain's decentralized and tamper-resistant nature makes it an ideal platform for various use cases, ranging from supply chain management and voting systems to tokenization and smart contracts. Its potential to revolutionize industries and enhance transparency and security has led to extensive research and development in the blockchain space.

Comparing cryptocurrencies to traditional fiat currencies highlighted the benefits and drawbacks of both systems. While cryptocurrencies offer borderless transactions, reduced fees, and financial inclusivity, they face challenges related to volatility, scalability, and regulatory uncertainties. Understanding these distinctions is crucial for making knowledgeable decisions and embracing the opportunities the crypto space presents.

A key takeaway from this book has been the importance of understanding cryptocurrency basics. This understanding empowers individuals to make informed investment decisions, secure their digital assets through wallets and private keys, and engage in trading and investment strategies. Moreover, grasping the concepts of decentralization, consensus mechanisms, and cryptographic security contributes to a more profound appreciation of the transformative potential of cryptocurrencies.

In exploring various types of cryptocurrencies, we encountered stablecoins - digital assets pegged to stable external assets, such as fiat currencies or commodities. Stablecoins offer stability, making them attractive for traders seeking to mitigate volatility risks. Additionally, we explored utility tokens and security tokens, each serving distinct purposes within blockchain ecosystems.

Storing and securing cryptocurrencies emerged as a critical topic in our discussions. We explored different types of wallets, such as hardware, software, and paper wallets, each offering varying degrees of security and convenience. Understanding public and private keys became essential for ensuring the safety of digital assets and avoiding potential security breaches.

We examined fundamental analysis, technical analysis, and market trends in cryptocurrency trading and investing. Understanding these analytical approaches equips traders and investors with tools to make informed decisions and navigate the complex and dynamic crypto market. Furthermore, we explored the environmental impact of mining and the emergence of alternative consensus mechanisms, such as proof-of-stake, offering more sustainable solutions.

Regulatory landscape and tax implications were crucial considerations in our journey. Regulatory clarity and compliance become vital for fostering a stable and secure stakeholder environment as the crypto space interacts with traditional financial systems and undergoes increasing institutional adoption.

Balancing the challenges and opportunities in the crypto space is an ongoing endeavor. Scalability, security, and financial inclusion are key areas for improvement. While DeFi and DAOs offer exciting opportunities for decentralized finance and governance, addressing their challenges, such as smart contract exploits and participation, is essential for sustainable growth.

As we conclude this book, we recognize that crypto remains a dynamic and evolving landscape. Emerging trends and technologies, including CBDCs, interoperability solutions, and decentralized governance, present further opportunities and challenges for the future.

In summary, our journey through this book has shed light on the intricate world of cryptocurrencies, their underlying technologies, and the strategies for navigating this exciting terrain. With the knowledge of key concepts and strategies, readers can embrace the transformative potential of cryptocurrencies, make knowledgeable decisions, and actively participate in the digital financial future. The crypto space's continued growth and evolution depend on collaboration, innovation, and responsible development, as we collectively shape the future of this paradigm-shifting revolution.

Encouragement to take the next steps in cryptocurrency journey

Congratulations! You have embarked on an exciting journey into the world of cryptocurrencies, unlocking the essential concepts and strategies that underpin this transformative technology. As you reach the conclusion of this book, it's natural to feel a mix of curiosity, enthusiasm, and perhaps even some trepidation about what lies ahead.

The first and most crucial step in your cryptocurrency journey is recognizing knowledge's power. By engaging with this book, you have already laid a strong foundation of understanding. However, cryptocurrencies are constantly evolving, and there is always more to learn. Stay curious, and seek out reputable sources of information to stay updated with the most current developments and trends. Continuously educating yourself about the nuances of the crypto space will empower you to make informed decisions and navigate the ever-changing landscape confidently.

Entering the crypto space might feel daunting, especially with the wealth of information and numerous digital assets available. It's essential to remember that you don't need to jump in headfirst. Start small, take measured steps, and familiarize yourself with the practical aspects of buying, selling, and trading cryptocurrencies. Many platforms offer demo accounts or test environments that allow you to practice without risking real money. Use these resources to gain hands-on experience and build your confidence as you explore the intricacies of the crypto market.

As you become more comfortable with cryptocurrencies, consider diversifying your portfolio. Cryptocurrencies come in various forms, each with unique characteristics and use cases. By diversifying, you spread risk and increase the potential for gains. Explore different types of digital assets, including cryptocurrencies, stablecoins, and utility tokens, to gain exposure to diverse sectors of the crypto market. Combine crypto assets with traditional investments to create a balanced and well-rounded portfolio.

Decentralized Finance, or DeFi, has emerged as a groundbreaking force in the crypto space, offering innovative financial services without intermediaries. Embrace the opportunities presented by DeFi protocols, such as lending, borrowing, and yield farming. Participating in DeFi not only opens new avenues for potential returns but also contributes to the growth and decentralization of the crypto ecosystem. However, exercise caution and conduct profound research before engaging with DeFi projects, as the space can be subject to risks.

While cryptocurrency trading can be exciting and rewarding, it's essential also to consider the benefits of long-term holding. Some digital assets have shown significant growth over time, rewarding patient investors. If you believe in the long-term potential of a particular cryptocurrency or blockchain project, holding your investments for the long haul can offer a unique perspective and potential for substantial returns.

Security should be a top priority in your cryptocurrency journey. Ensure you store your digital assets in secure wallets, and keep your private keys safe and protected. Beware of phishing attempts and scams that target unsuspecting individuals in the crypto space. Always verify the authenticity of websites, projects, and individuals before sharing any sensitive information. By adopting best security practices, you can protect your investments and have peace of mind while navigating the crypto landscape.

Beyond investing and trading, consider exploring the underlying technology of cryptocurrencies - blockchain. The potential use cases of blockchain technology extend far beyond digital assets. Blockchain can revolutionize various industries from supply chain management and healthcare to voting systems and intellectual property protection. Embrace the technological revolution and explore the myriad possibilities for blockchain adoption and innovation.

The crypto space is more than just an investment opportunity; it's a vibrant and passionate community of like-minded individuals. Engage with the crypto community through forums, social media, and local meetups. Engage in discussion, pose questions, and share your perspectives. As you embrace the future of finance together, you can obtain insightful ideas, learn from the experiences of others in the crypto field, and experience a sense of camaraderie.

Finally, remember that the crypto journey is a continuous learning experience. Embrace the ups and downs, the challenges, and the triumphs. Be open to adapting your strategies, learning from your mistakes, and celebrating your successes. The crypto space is dynamic and ever-changing, and your journey will be one of growth and exploration.

In conclusion, your cryptocurrency journey holds boundless potential. Armed with knowledge, curiosity, and a willingness to engage, you can navigate the complexities of the crypto space and embrace the future of finance. Whether you invest, trade, or explore the technological aspects of blockchain, the opportunities are vast. As you take the following steps in your cryptocurrency journey, remember to stay informed, exercise caution, and embrace the transformative potential of this digital financial frontier. The future is in your hands - so take that leap and embrace the exciting world of cryptocurrencies!

Thank you for buying and reading/ listening to our book. If you found this book useful/ helpful please take a few minutes and leave a review on the platform where you purchased our book. Your feedback matters greatly to us.